Our Decentralized Literature

Our Decentralized Literature

Cultural Mediations in Selected

Jewish and Southern Writers

Jules Chametzky

The University of Massachusetts Press

Amherst, 1986

Copyright © 1986 by The University of Massachusetts Press
All rights reserved
Printed in the United States of America
Set in Linoterm Janson at The University of Massachusetts Press
Printed by Cushing-Malloy and bound by John Dekker & Sons

Library of Congress Cataloging-in-Publication Data

Chametzky, Jules.
Our decentralized literature.

Includes index.
1. American literature—Jewish authors—History and criticism—
Addresses, essays, lectures. 2. American literature—Southern States—
History and criticism—Addresses, essays, lectures. 3. Jews in
literature—Addresses, essays, lectures. I. Title.
PS153.J4C46   1986   810'.9'8924   86–1259
ISBN 0–87023–527–3 (alk. paper)
ISBN 0–87023–540–0 (pbk.: alk. paper)

For Anne, Matthew, Robert, Peter

Contents

Acknowledgments

All of the essays in this collection have been previously published. I am grateful to the various editors and publishers for permission to reprint them. In a few cases their titles are slightly different from the originals. My numerous scholarly and personal debts are evident in the texts and footnotes.

"Our Decentralized Literature: A Consideration of Regional, Ethnic, Racial, and Sexual Factors," *Jahrbuch für Amerikastudien* 17 (Heidelberg, 1972): 56–72.

"Notes on the Assimilation of the American-Jewish Writer: Abraham Cahan to Saul Bellow," *Jahrbuch für Amerikastudien* 9 (Heidelberg, 1964): 173–80.

"Immigrant Fiction as Cultural Mediation," *Modern Jewish Studies Annual* 5 (Fall 1984): 14–21.

"History in I. B. Singer's Novels," in *Critical Views of Isaac B. Singer*, ed. I. Malin (New York: New York University Press, 1969), pp. 169–77.

"Edward Dahlberg, Early and Late," in *Proletarian Writers of the Thirties*, ed. David Madden (Carbondale, Ill.: Southern Illinois University Press, 1968), pp. 64–73.

"Elmer Rice, Liberation, and the Great Ethnic Question," in *From Hester Street to Hollywood*, ed. Sarah B. Cohen (Bloomington: Indiana University Press, 1983), pp. 71–84.

"Realism, Cultural Politics, and Language As Mediation in Mark Twain and Others," *Prospects* 8 (Cambridge and New York: Cambridge University Press, 1983), pp. 183–96.

"Thomas Wolfe: The Writer and His Experience," in *The Modern Temper: Society and Culture in 20th Century America* (Cologne: Amerika Haus, 1963), pp. 99–111.

"Styron's *Sophie's Choice*, Jews and Other Marginals, and the Mainstream," *Prospects* 9 (Cambridge and New York: Cambridge University Press, 1984), pp. 433–40.

Our Decentralized Literature

Introduction

In the last paragraph of Chinua Achebe's *Things Fall Apart*—perhaps the most memorable account in English of an African culture and the impact upon it of white European encroachment—the voice and language of the book shifts with startling abruptness. From the point of view of a sensibility deep within tribal culture—in which the reader has been privileged throughout the novel to participate and whose world has therefore become familiar, nuanced, rich, and real as lived experience can be—we are suddenly forced to see all that fullness reduced by the language of the conqueror. As he orders the body of Okonkwo cut down from the tree, the English district commissioner reflects on his plans to write a book about his years toiling to bring "civilization to different parts of Africa." He muses, "The story of this man who had killed a messenger and hanged himself would make interesting reading. One could almost write a whole chapter on him. Perhaps not a whole chapter but a reasonable paragraph, at any rate. There was so much else to include, and one must be firm in cutting out details. He had already chosen the title of the book, after much thought: *The Pacification of the Primitive Tribes of the Lower Niger.*"

Anyone who has read or taught this novel can testify to the outrageous reductionism of this last paragraph, especially its last sentence. It is chilling, but ultimately fulfills the enlightening effort of the whole book. Obviously, it forces us to confront the "Rashomon" aspect of experience—that things look different to different observers, and that one's very perceptions are shaped by the social and cultural context out of which one operates. More significantly for my purposes, and from the perspective of a chief assumption underlying this collection of essays written over a span of more than twenty years, is the demonstration, brutal and unmistakable in this case, that who controls, or attempts to control, language and the act of interpretation—the process of naming and definition—aims to control in imperial fashion historic memory, culture, and people.[1]

By "taking the words out of their mouths," as it were, and substituting their own words, cultural dominance of a particular group, class, nation—hegemony, to use the currently fashionable term—is established and legitimated. The struggle to retain or recover or invent out of an acculturated existence her- and histories involves over and over again the recovery of a voice, the articulated embodiment of experience that is authentically and legitimately one's own. I speak of "an acculturated existence," by which I mean taking into account the historic reality for many people and groups of submission or subordination to dominant cultural ideals. This condition frequently resulted in internalizing those ideals and therefore having to deal with or mediate the kind of "doubleness" W. E. B. Du Bois talked of in *The Souls of Black Folk*:

> It is a peculiar sensation, this double-consciousness, this sense of always looking at one's self through the eyes of others. . . . One ever feels his twoness—an American, a Negro; two souls, two thoughts, two unreconciled strivings; two warring ideals in one dark body, whose dogged strength alone keeps it from being torn asunder. [(New York: Fawcett, 1961), pp. 16–17]

Every Jew in Christendom, every woman in a male-dominated world, every Southerner (or Westerner) in the United States, every person of color in a racist society, knows there are at least two answers to every question. This simple home truth can be stated more abstractly and theoretically as recognizing the central particularities of existence that shape a voice of one's own (to paraphrase Virginia Woolf): the elements of our social and cultural existence we have learned with less embarrassment over two decades to identify as racial, sexual, ethnic, and regional factors. It

1. See the editor's note to a translation of the profound essay on Kafka developing this idea, by Gilles Deleuze and Félix Guattari, "What Is a Minor Literature?" *Mississippi Review* 22, 3 (Spring 1983): 13–33.

is not as fashionable as it once was to consider class, though that is a factor frequently subsumed by or interacting with the others.

The essay given pride of place in this collection, "Our Decentralized Literature: The Significance of Regional, Ethnic, Racial, and Sexual Factors," deals precisely with this question. It sets the framework for Part I of the book, called "Controlling Language and Culture" (the ambiguity and doubleness of the title is obviously deliberate). The aim is to provide a largely theoretical overview, although in the form of concrete analyses of specific passages and texts. (The habits of a New Critical graduate training, albeit within a general American Studies approach, die hard.) The issues dealt with in this essay will be touched upon in almost every essay in the book, most obviously in the last section on Southern writers.

One's own vision and voice are shaped by the special history and normative patterns of rhetoric and thought of a region and a landscape; by the race, gender, and ethnic group one is born into; and with varying degrees of intensity, depending on the vagaries of history and social circumstance, one's ultimate fate. When, as is often the case in our culture, matters of such magnitude are relegated to positions of so-called marginality, or to mere accident or inconsequentiality in the larger quest for literary "excellence," "centrality," or "universality," there is clearly a serious distortion at work, a serious effort at appropriation and control. As Jane Tompkins has recently shown in her important study of the cultural and historical contexts that condition all writing and criticism, such control is exercised by dominant institutional networks of shared values, critical assumptions, and power.[2]

I am pleased that the main title of the first essay, "Our Decentralized Literature," comes from an essay written in 1899 by William Dean Howells. The uses I put it to, however, are appropriate to a post-Foucauldian awareness that "decentering" and deconstructing presumably fixed and coherent structures of meaning are a necessary prelude to less imperial approaches to knowledge and understanding. In that essay I examine how significant writers were misinterpreted, and in effect thereby silenced, by

2. Jane Tompkins, *Sensational Designs: The Cultural Work of American Fiction, 1790–1860* (New York: Oxford University Press, 1985).

dominant and prevailing approaches to their work. I express the hope, there and here, that in our time we are better equipped to read their meanings as well as their letters. We can now see their true concerns and the special quality of their mediations between a dominant set of cultural values and perceptions of experience and a presumably less central one. In the process, we can apprehend, I believe, the transformation in our own consciousness of the marginal to the central. That is a rather extraordinary story, touched upon in one form or another throughout this collection of essays.

The second essay, "The Assimilation of the American Jewish Writer: Abraham Cahan to Saul Bellow," confronts more directly the question of language. In those watershed decades at the turn of the century when the United States was assuming its decidedly modern characteristics, Howells and James knew that this was indeed a central question, having to do with literary reputation, self-definition, and power. The problem is seen in the context of "the ethnic question," a subject central to more than half the essays in this book. At the end of the 1950s, the Jewish part in American letters was beginning to be seen as a major one, so the occasion for such an exploration was highly appropriate. In that essay I trace the development of Jewish writers from a dominated to a liberated "ethnic" voice evident in the work of ground-breaking Jewish American writers from Abraham Cahan to Saul Bellow. At the time I may have been the first critic to place Cahan so conspicuously at the beginning of the astonishing development of a Jewish American literature, a theme I developed more fully a few years later in a book on Cahan's entire fictional output in both English and Yiddish.[3] Having thus helped to establish Cahan as "Father of world of our fathers" (to quote the title of a review of the Cahan book in *Partisan Review*), I regret, and here take the opportunity to apologize for, omitting a treatment of the mothers in the equally astonishing development of a Jewish American women's literature. In an article not included in this collection, because it is largely a chronicle of names, dates, brief synopses, and thumbnail social

3. Jules Chametzky, *From the Ghetto: The Fiction of Abraham Cahan* (Amherst: University of Massachusetts Press, 1977).

and intellectual histories that are replicated elsewhere in the present text, I do make mention of and honor the achievement of these mothers—Emma Lazarus, Mary Antin, Anzia Yezierska—and some of the numerous women writers who followed in their paths (Lillian Hellman, Grace Paley, Cynthia Ozick, Adrienne Rich, Erica Jong, Tillie Olsen, Helen Yglesias).[4]

In the second essay, the issues raised by the supposed pattern of liberation are tied consciously to specific historic and social circumstances in the life of American Jews. This seems to me the most productive road to understanding and even evaluating writers, despite our American infatuation with the idea of the heroic individual and solitary effort, or the notion of the singular writer of genius who creates only out of an imagination that at its best owes little or nothing to the world around him. As Deleuze and Guattari have pointed out, this is especially true of minority writers—that is, those writers whose work exists on the "margin" of a "major" culture. The efforts of such writers, correctly read, are attempts to avoid "deterritorialization." Their work is therefore always political—concerned with power relationships—even when it concerns the Oedipal complex.[5] This is not to say, however, that the individual or the singular writer does not exist or does not matter. That would be absurd.

Most writers of note, certainly those I consider significant mediators between various audiences and cultures that are part of America's evolving reality, are those who display unusual acuity and frequent audacity in transforming the latent materials of their time into manifest utterance. Many are called, few are chosen. Few become Mark Twain, or Saul Bellow, or Harriet Beecher Stowe, or William Faulkner, who by their work and its reception change the language and culture. These considerations touch upon the third of the chief and deeply interrelated concerns of the essays that follow: the first of these concerns is language; the second, ethnic and regional factors (exemplary of significant "particularities") as central rather than marginal aspects of twentieth-century

4. "Main Currents in American Jewish Literature from the 1880s to the 1950s (and beyond)," *Ethnic Groups* 4, 1 & 2 (1982): 85–101.

5. Deleuze and Guattari, "What Is a Minor Literature?" pp. 16–17.

American culture; and the third, the role and strategy of the "marginal" writer as he/she struggles with these elements within the wider cultural context. In the process, the writer transforms all the elements, re-creating or re-presenting them imaginatively and symbolically so that a new self, expressed in a new and compelling voice, stands at the center of that world we call culture. That is the burden of the long essay on Mark Twain, and the shorter one on William Styron that closes the collection, and will explain the high prototypical role assigned to Twain and to Philip Roth—about which there is more later in this introduction.

For now, I shall return to the second essay in the book, "The Assimilation of the American Jewish Writer," and the issues raised by the supposed pattern of liberation I discerned in the development of the Jewish American literary voice. Although related importantly to the specifics of the historical development of the Jewish situation in America over several decades, I suggested that the pattern was paradigmatic for American writers generally. Such a view might at first seem paradoxical, if not a flat contradiction. What I asserted, which is related to the discussion above about the nature of the American writer, is that I believed we had reached a point at which the ethnic writer, like the Southern or Catholic writer before him/her, could now be seen without self-consciousness as "the American writer."

My views may have been premature in one respect, prescient in another. I called for a turn toward the authentic materials of one's experience as the basis for a new literary constellation, but obviously could not predict the strength of the so-called ethnic revival of the late sixties and seventies, which is, even now, in full tilt—although its end, at least in some of the forms it has recently taken, seems to me in sight. To encapsulate such a broad social phenomenon in a few sentences is difficult, but much is available on the subject, much has been told to a fare-thee-well, so a few sentences should suffice. In addition to some of the same elements operating in the Jewish situation—the need to affirm a part of the self that escaped defining by the mainstream, and a position of enough social security and support to make it possible—there was the urgency of the civil rights and black awareness movements of the sixties that produced a generation of new writers to extend the pioneering work of Wright, Ellison, and Baldwin. This provided a powerful stimulus to self-assertion among Hispanic, Native American, and Asian writers and their public. Among so-called white ethnics, the rediscovery of the pluralistic nature of American culture produced similarly self-conscious and assertive ethnic identification.

This development has been on the whole a positive and enriching one, quite in line with most of the assumptions and positions I have taken in this book. We are now more aware of the diversity in America's past, the multiethnic nature of its culture, the dangers of a narrowly conceived ethnocentrism. On the other hand, we have seen the emergence of what Werner Sollors has called "ethnic insiderism," occasionally allied to an insidious kind of biological insiderism, that tends to forget the Americanness of so much of American ethnicity. The critic who argues that only a black critic can interpret or evaluate black writing; or only a Jewish intellectual of a certain urban background can appreciate *Portnoy's Complaint;* or, as argued at a meeting of the Modern Languages Association a few years ago, that only an Italian could fully understand all the nuances of *The Godfather*, is surely mistaken—replacing an old orthodoxy with a new one. To present the Beat movement, for example, as a congeries of ethnic writers—Kerouac as Franco-American, O'Hara as Irish, Ginsburg as Jewish, Jones/Baraka as Afro-American, and so on—is surely to miss the forest for a stage-set of trees.[6]

All of these examples, and more, represent important parts of an American literature and an American culture. Their borrowings from each other, their connectedness to and similarities with other strands in the complex mosaic of our culture (I deliberately eschew the terms "alembic" and "melting pot"), can only be understood in an American context. There are no fixed, metaphysical absolutes for ethnic consciousness and the forms it will take. These forms and the work they do for their producers and consumers (and here, again, I refer to Jane Tompkins's important insights), are time con-

6. For the references to *The Godfather* and the Beats, I am indebted to the introduction in Werner Sollors, *Beyond Ethnicity: Consent and Descent in American Culture* (New York: Oxford University Press, 1986).

ditioned, historically conditioned, socially conditioned. I happen to think this work is and has been very important, but when one of its phases seems completed, it is time to move ahead intellectually, as ethnic consciousness itself does, to confront new problems in our evolving social reality.

So, in the final essay of the first section, "Immigrant Fiction as Cultural Mediation," I attempt another overview, with the object of seeing the situation from a reasonably contemporary perspective. In some ways the essay is a reprise of many elements in the earlier essays, focusing again on questions of language, but fully cognizant now of more than a decade of revisionist Marxist thought that complicates older notions of fictional representation, the emergence of reader-response and implied reader criticism, and a more assured and sophisticated ethnic and social history. From these perspectives—to which I would add Deleuze's and Guattari's perception that minority literatures evade or offer alternatives to mainstream criticism and are available to critical acts by anyone with that awareness, not just kin—it becomes clear that filial-pietistic and naively chauvinist approaches should be abandoned. It is in this light that my focus on Philip Roth as an exemplary figure should be understood.

When Zuckerman's father, with what is practically his dying breath, calls him "Bastard!", who knows but that on some level he speaks to and for us all, despite the very specific circumstances motivating and conditioning the utterance, as Ellison's anonymous black narrator concludes *he* may be doing at the end of *Invisible Man*. The fatherless child, or one abandoned by or abandoning, or denied by or denying, a father (the traditional source of authority and a potent past) is a pervasive motif in the American literary canon. It derives its resonance, no doubt, from the quintessentially American gesture, rooted in history and sanctioned by myth, of transoceanic rebirth in the New World, overcoming the domination of a King and Divine Right, abandoning the physical sites of Fatherland and Mother Church.

One of the essays cites Augie March as taking his place in the line of literary heroes who are symbolically or literally fatherless or wholly orphaned. Another focuses on Edward Dahlberg's artist as a young man needing somehow to come to terms with his patrimony (and in which the Oedipal struggle is converted to one of achieving, finally, an American identity). As noted earlier, the ethnic situation adds this special dimension to the Oedipal one by embodying these political or broadly cultural implications. Like Hamlet, the ethnic son (or daughter, as Yezierska's *Bread Givers* forcefully reminds us) is often forced to attend the voice of his dead or dying father calling from beyond the grave, "Remember me!" In *Yekl*, the hero Jake is recalled by news of his father's death back to what had already become for him a somewhat dreamlike place, "The Old Country," to a sense of the old values that he seemed happily on the way to abandoning. "In the grip of his past," as Cahan entitles the chapter describing this process, Jake is enjoined to assume his role as *paterfamilias*—no more dating dance-hall girls and assuming Yankee attitudes. Zuckerman is cursed by his father for traducing and abandoning the ancient verities regarding sex (he's written a best-selling book about an inveterate masturbator and *shikse*-chaser), ethnic and familial loyalties and secrets, the values of the old neighborhood.

This call of the past has emotive and psychological power, although its hold is evidently transient: ultimately, Jake divorces the *shtetl* wife of his youth (who herself goes on to change formidably in the American ambience) and marries one of the dance-hall girls; loaded with guilt, Zuckerman nevertheless cuts himself loose and goes on to "The Prague Orgy"—much as his literary alter-ego, "The Professor of Desire," goes on a quest for Kafka's whore (an unorthodox search for "roots"). This kind of decoding of such prototypical narratives suggests much, I believe, about ethnic consciousness, certainly in the recent period of the ethnic revival. Such a consciousness is an effort to keep alive—or create, in some instances—a real or imagined Old World or pre-American Home and its values as a sacred space, as it were. If that past has receded irrecoverably or become too dreamlike or ghostly, an Old Neighborhood, region, territory and its values, within America itself, is affirmed against the encroachment of the profane values of the general American world. The form of these affirmations (visits to the old neighborhood, eating ethnic food) is frequently more symbolic than real when seen against the enormous pressures of a fluid but powerful American reality, as Herbert Gans has shown.[7] Still, the need to act out the rituals is a revealing one. Roth's special value, in these respects, lies in his unerring aim at certain literary conventions and ethnic or cultural pieties that prevent the writer from honestly confronting and suitably chronicling his times and his experience of it. When he kills his literary mother and father, as at points in these essays I suggest he does, it does not mean he does not like or honor his real mother and father. This picture of a pipe is not a pipe. Seemingly denigrating a past—more accurately, usually a set of literary conventions—he is actually affirming its strength as he works to liberate himself from its smothering effects upon the creative imagination. He is not evading the particularities of his experience, which are in fact a productive element in the dialectic between past and present that will free him for further struggle in the future with those old and new ghosts that always haunt writers and cultures.

In this respect there is a link between Roth and I. B. Singer, at least as I conceive a certain aspect of Singer's work in "History in I. B. Singer's Novels," the essay that opens Part II. Both writers answer the ghostly call of the past, neither is uncritical or paralyzed by its pieties or power, both assure its continued life in the world of imagination.

Singer is, of course, the most unmistakably Jewish writer of our times. He writes in Yiddish, a Jewish language, always about Jewish characters, immersed in the specifics of Jewish history and fate. Yet there is a hovering aura about his work that can only be called mythic. What is he doing in a book about American literature and culture? Aside from the fact that he has been an American citizen for more than forty years and lived in this country since 1935, his work and career dramatically exemplify several matters with which this book is concerned.

7. Herbert J. Gans, "Symbolic Ethnicity: The Future of Ethnic Groups and Cultures in America," in *On the Making of Americans: Essays in Honor of David Riesman*, ed. Herbert J. Gans et al. (Philadelphia: University of Pennsylvania Press, 1979), pp. 193–220. See also Allen Guttmann's fine discussion of these issues in *The Jewish Writer in America* (New York: Oxford University Press, 1971).

First is the extraordinary way he shows that working through the specifics and the particular—even in a presumably minor language or voice—at the outermost margin of apparently mainstream concerns, is no bar to acceptance as a generally relevant and major voice. A Nobel Prize in literature is no sure sign of that, but in the absence of other measurable contemporary criteria, it will have to do. His relation to language is also instructive: Yiddish has been called a dying language, to which Singer's set reply has been, "Let me remind you, ladies and gentlemen, dying is not dead." So long as a major writer uses a tongue, people will have to learn it—which is another way of observing, once again, that writers keep alive or revivify language. In this case that old bromide has a poignant historic meaning. Yiddish was the language of the overwhelming majority of the victims of the Holocaust, central to who they were, their way-of-being-in-the-world, the language with which they went to their deaths. Keeping it alive is an act of homage, of restoration, and of resistance to that nearly successful effort to expunge Jewish existence. Singer's is an act of solidarity with and an awareness of a specifically Jewish fate and a gesture toward its mythic capacity to renew itself, despite, as I will point out, Singer's appreciation of the crushing and implacable forces of history.

Most writers operate somewhere along the intersection of history and myth as I define these concepts. History is the dynamic powerhouse (to use Philip Rahv's well-known formulation) of events and change that emphasizes the transitory, relative, and more than individual dimension of experience; myth is the effort to embrace feeling and meaning through the stories, missions, and notions of special origins and fates with which people and nations invest themselves and with which they confront or seek to evade the powerhouse.

The three essays in Part II, which I call "History, Myth, and the Ethnic Question," may be seen as three strategies in this encounter. Singer, as has been asserted, displays the most extremely "ethnic" approach; Dahlberg is a Jewish writer, at least as I note the fact in "Edward Dahlberg: The Jewish Orphan in America," who opts to embrace various nonethnic myths in the search for the universal—from a bottom-dog world and its rude vernacular to that of the artist, the American, and finally to classic mythology and the highest style; Rice may be seen as the epitome of the assimilated American writer, who opts for the universality of the Enlightenment, but who is forced to confront, not with the center of his work or being, however, an inescapable connection with Jewish fate and history. Insofar as he does that, I argue in the essay called "Elmer Rice, Liberation, and the Great Ethnic Question," then Rice's work has a living center: insofar as he evades it, Dahlberg's work threatens to leave this world entirely for a place where style is all, and he may well prove to be the sport of American letters I argue in the essay he might not be. Singer starts out as an oddity, a kind of "sport," who by working through the particulars of a very Jewish existence achieves what looks like a universal dimension—a position and strategy he shares, for the most part, with other sports like Achebe, Bellow, and Faulkner.

In the discussion of Rice's *Counsellor-at-Law*, I use the phrase, "the confrontation of ethnic outsider and dominant culture," which touches upon a subject relevant to an earlier discussion of the three-generational development of the ethnic American writer. It is relevant as well to concerns that antedate and in a sense subsume ethnic themes—or at least give us a context in which we can see these broaden to become part of enduring myth/history confrontations. A recurring motif throughout histories, chronicles, and literatures is the challenge to elites and controlling powers by energetic outsiders from the provinces, or from the lower classes, or barbarians, or racial and ethnic "others." Depending on the point of view, the center may be seen as suffering from waning energy, decadence, or desuetude, and must be renewed, defended, or taken over. In a wonderful essay that introduces James's *Princess Casamassima*, Lionel Trilling talks about the prevalence of the theme in nineteenth-century fiction of "the young man from the province": the outsider or upstart who attempts to storm the central city or place of power, Paris, and with it all of Europe. Trilling cites the historical fact of Napoleon as the basis for the continuing fascination of this theme.[8] Despite that, the recurrence of such a narrative in stories and myths of various times and places un-

8. Lionel Trilling, *The Liberal Imagination* (New York: Doubleday, 1950), pp. 55–88.

doubtedly embraces a world of feeling and emotion as much as "objective" historical fact. We saw such emotion expended by Henry James in *The American Scene*, when he dealt with and coined the phrase, "the great ethnic question." James may have been echoing or giving expression to a barely repressed curse by others of his class and situation when confronting the challenge of these swarming hordes of outsiders. In the fullness of time and from a more secure social position, and with intellectual *chutzpah*, those whose ancestors were cursed seized the metaphor and converted it to their own mythic purposes, with pride. Rice touches upon these issues, but never goes far enough, as my essay argues, and thereby forfeits an opportunity to achieve more than he did.

If Rice subscribes only unconsciously, or opportunistically, to this mythic source of energy (strong ethnic versus effete aristocracy), Edward Dahlberg consciously embraces myths of large and heroic dimension—from the American Ishmael to Oedipus and the world of classic mythology. By a leap of language and convention, he seeks to leave the world of bottom-dog and marginal outsider for the centrality of a world-embracing consciousness. Or is he simply one more "ethnic" trying through the madness of art to leap out of his skin, evade his fate, and refuse to mediate his doubleness? Dahlberg was part of the important movement to legitimize the "rude vernacular" that made possible Bellow, Roth, and so many others, but his rejection of it and its implications was total (as was his "nonidentifying" as a Jew). Cut off in this way, he inhabited, too often, only the airy realm of heightened language. Lizzie Lewis, like Bellow's Grandma Lausch, is where the vitality and the real emotion were. Without such a concrete center, or the strong memory of one, his style could become vaporous, floating toward empyrean realms. I hate to be so judgmental, but perhaps, finally, despite the singular triumph as style of *Because I Was Flesh*, Edward Dahlberg's career is a kind of cautionary tale. One must seek the universal through particulars, not lay it on with a trowel.

To some extent, that is what I imply parenthetically in the Styron piece—"Styron's *Sophie's Choice:* Jews and Other Marginals," which is the final essay of Part III, "The Southerner as All-American Writer"—and when I refer to the heavy freight he carries with talk of sin and Auschwitz, although the situation, and

Styron's intentions, as well as my own, are more complicated. These intentions, as should be abundantly clear by now, have to do with a rethinking of the constituents of an American literary culture. The process includes attending receptively to the diverse voices of our culture, understanding always the lines of development within and between them, and respecting the social and historical context.

Early in the book I call attention to the social meanings of Howells's psychological and literary ambivalences. These have to do with defining a place for one's self, as writer and person, within the shifting class, regional, ethnic, and professional relationships of American life. This idea is picked up in the essay, "Realism, Cultural Politics, and Language as Mediation in Mark Twain," in my view one of the most important in this collection. Here, Howells appears again, as a spokesperson for literary realism and an arbiter of cultural judgment. It should be clear that no literary judgment is value-free, or anything less than self-legitimating, as is evident in the terms of Howells's acceptance of Cahan's vision and language. A similar process is at work in Styron's treatment of the chief contenders for a central place in the culture of his time, who are not too different from those of Howells's: Southern forebears, Jewish writers of clear significance, blacks, and women.

In this section, I am not attempting to show the self-interest of a Southern constituency, but rather to suggest once more the Americanness of this enterprise of defining the ground on which one stands as *the* native ground, the meaningful place and center of an authentic American self. The subtlety of Styron's achievement, like Twain's and Roth's, lies in the awareness that the ground tends to shift, is not a fixed place, in time or geography, ethnically or any other way, but rather depends on the flexibility, wit, and awareness of the writer as adapter and projector of various mediations and negotiations.

Twain's great image of the Mississippi as a text and as a paradigm of America, and the writer as a pilot negotiating its inveterate changes, is the key to the process. Beginning in the period of realism, I believe, the writer assumes an interesting social role within American life generally. He/she is increasingly treated as someone whose life itself becomes of more interest than the work he/she produces. This occurs because that life is seen as an example of autonomy and of unalienated work, possibilities that are under dire threat of extinction in all other areas of public life in the era of late capitalism. Twain's lavish attention to the riverboat pilot's autonomy as the last and greatest independent power on earth should be understood, as I have presented the equation, as referring to the writer in America. That is an elevated role, indeed. It may account for Twain's feeling that he, too, may be an imposter, but it also emphasizes the process of the writer's self-creation within a field of social imperatives. Jay Gatsby, né Gatz, that prototypical believer in the American Dream—who thought he could create a Platonic conception of himself whole out of his imagination—sought to abolish the past and rewrite it all according to his own conception. It is a compelling vision, but a flawed and fatal one, as we know. Twain and many of the writers discussed in this book share one part of the Dream: that the creation of an American self is open to all with audacity, imagination, and the luck to be at the right place at the right time. But the Dream must be tempered with the sober knowledge bequeathed us by pilot Twain: heed the rocks and the real currents when you follow the green light at the end of the dock. One carries an imagined conception of the River in mind—indeed, one must when running in darkness or foul weather—but that imagination, too, is the product of a deep experience of its formidable and lengthy particulars.

With these considerations in mind, the inclusion of the essay "Thomas Wolfe and the Cult of Experience" can be better understood. I would like, as well, to help restore his once high place in the American literary canon. Wolfe is still read, of course, by young people, drunk—as he often seemed to be—on the richness and potential of America and its language. However, among "serious" critics he is often an embarrassment. I do not want to review the history of our literary criticism in recent decades, or the frequently social and political assumptions underlying its positions. It simply strikes me, in the context of this book and its arguments, that Wolfe may have been the first Southern writer to be widely regarded as the authentic Great American Writer, speaking in his yawps and lists like Whitman for the whole amazing panorama. His work, like much else in the thirties, legitimated regionals, ethnics, bottom-dog "others," marginals of all kinds. His storming of the citadels of culture in the period between the wars preceded and made possible, I would argue, the ultimate perception of writers such as Faulkner and Robert Penn Warren as major American voices.

As a final introductory word, I want to testify personally to the singular importance of William Faulkner, his work and its reception, to all who concern themselves with the issues raised in these essays. For two years in the 1950s, while still a graduate student, I was coeditor of a small journal called *Faulkner Studies*, engaging in, along with many others, what a friend at the time called "Talmudic Faulknerism." That jesting reference still reverberates for me. My interest in how the provincial and regional may be transformed into the major and the universal began with that involvement; more interesting to me now is the striking way it illustrates how presumed boundaries of cultural separateness are crossed and influence one another in the wonderfully variegated patterns of American life and culture.

Such crossings of boundaries for the wider enrichment of the whole go on all the time, of course. My last words in the Styron essay that concludes this volume are that blacks and women are "on the threshold of real entry to and possession of their share of the center of our collective American lives." Now one should be able to say they have crossed over that threshold and firmly occupy that central position which is their due. But that is the subject of another book.

Amherst
July 1985

I

Controlling Language and
Culture

One

Our Decentralized Literature:

The Significance of Regional, Ethnic, Racial,

and Sexual Factors

INTRODUCTION

The topic presented for our discussion at this meeting is Regionalism, but I have chosen to broaden the subject along the lines in my title, for reasons I hope to make clear in a moment. My basic assumption about "regionalism" stems from a suggestion of Larzer Ziff's in his indispensable study of *The American 1890s:* that the celebration of local color and regionalism in American literature became, in certain circumstances, toward the end of the nineteenth century a strategy, largely, for ignoring or minimizing social issues of great significance.[1] These issues concerned race and class and the new money power; an upheaval in American ethnic composition; far-reaching challenges to older American social assumptions and mores. Such matter called for serious literary treatment; but such matter deeply explored could upset notions of a unified national culture. Local color and regional literature could be accepted

A lecture presented at the Annual Meeting of the German American Studies Association, 4 June 1971. I want to thank Professors Ursula Brumm and T. A. Riese for their invitation to speak before the association, and Dr. Robert Gottwald, Renate Rott, and Werner Sollors, colleagues at the John F. Kennedy-Institut für Amerikastudien, for their help and advice in the preparation of this paper.

1. Larzer Ziff, *The American 1890s: Life and Times of a Lost Generation* (New York: Viking Press, 1968), p. 18.

in acknowledgment of the new diversity everywhere apparent in American life in this era of "historical change unprecedented to a degree,"[2] but the dominant public, and leading editors, would accept them only insofar as they reinforced notions of a basically homogeneous rather than a conflicted nation and culture. When Howells used the phrase "our decentralized literature" in an 1899 article,[3] he was acknowledging a fact of our literary and national life, but by giving it a largely geographic significance (as he did), he was minimizing a graver possibility: that of a lost center (defined as, where *he* had long stood) to American culture generally.

Against this background, I want to examine some works, and to some extent the careers, of four writers who were accepted—critically or popularly—as regional or local color writers of considerable achievement, but who were misunderstood, misrepresented, or totally denied, in what we may now see as their significant concerns. The four, roughly contemporaneous, are George Washington Cable (who starts somewhat earlier than the others), Abraham Cahan, Charles Chesnutt, and Kate Chopin. All of them were at one time thought to be regionalists and, indeed, still are so categorized in some literary histories, but their real subjects are, respectively: the racial grounds of the Southern tragedy, the stakes involved in the acculturation of immigrant populations, the assertion of a black ethos, and the terms of woman's entrapment within our cultural assumptions. A mere listing of these subjects suggests the contemporary relevance of these writers, a relevance to which I will allude but will not belabor in the course of this essay—it is more properly the subject of more extended treatment. It might also suggest why the dominant middle-class public at the moment of America's "modern" emergence could not or would not appreciate these writers in their true concerns—*that* is a subject to which I will more than allude. The denial of these concerns ultimately weakened or silenced Cable, Cahan, Chesnutt, and Chopin. To some extent, my chief purpose is to reexamine and

2. Warner Berthoff, *The Ferment of Realism, 1884–1919* (New York: Free Press, 1965), p. 12.

3. W. D. Howells, *Literature and Life* (New York: Harper and Bros., 1902), p. 177.

present freshly these very good and sometimes excellent writers in
their uniqueness and importance.

GEORGE WASHINGTON CABLE

In the opening chapter of his book, Ziff discusses a public reading
given during two days in 1887 in New York for the benefit of the
American Copyright League by what were at the time undoubtedly "the chief representatives of American literature."[4] Among the
participants were James Russell Lowell, Oliver Wendell Holmes,
John Greenleaf Whittier, Mark Twain, Edward Eggleston, Richard Henry Stoddard, James Whitcomb Riley, George Washington
Cable (all of them, it should be parenthetically noted, White,
Anglo-Saxon, Protestant, Male: a kind of homogeneity despite
their differences). Ziff writes:

> The kind of literature represented . . . was one which was regional
> in its tone and setting but national in its moral purpose and in its
> shared sentiments. The admission of geographical differences in-
> herent in the exploitation of local color had developed into an ignor-
> ing of deeper social differences. Insofar as these differences were
> a subject for literature, the burden was the underlying goodhearted
> humanity of all men regardless of background, when faced with the
> important matters of courtship, children, and age.[5]

That seemed to be all the facts, when you got to brass tacks (to
paraphrase T. S. Eliot)—or those were all the facts the audiences
wanted to hear, apparently; the audiences during those two days in
New York, at least, were "large and enthusiastic."

One of the stars of the occasion was George Washington Cable.
As Ziff puts it,

> his uncanny ability to communicate the lilt of Creole dialect on the
> printed page as well as from the lecture platform had brought him in
> 1887 to the peak of his fame, a fame which was exceeded only by that
> of his contemporary, [James Whitcomb] Riley, singer of Hoosier
> songs and Hoosier sentiments.[6]

4. Ziff, *The American 1890s*, p. 15.   6. Ibid., p. 7.
5. Ibid., p. 18.

In an entirely different context, a few years later (in 1898), review-
ing a volume of stories by Abraham Cahan, Howells said these
stories bore

> the same topographical relation to the East Side of New York
> that Miss [Mary E.] Wilkins bears to New England, or Miss [Ann]
> Nicholas to Indiana [*An Idyll of the Wabash and Other Stories*], or
> Miss [Lilian] Bell's [*The Instinct of Step-Fatherhood*] to the South, or
> Mr. [David] Gray's [*Gallops*] to Western New York.[7]

The year after this review, in a piece in the *Times Literary Supplement* intended to explain "our decentralized literature" to the English, Howells lumped Cahan among other "New York Writers"—
namely Richard Harding Davis, Brander Matthews, Frank
Norris.[8]

Now these links with other writers, and to a saleable subject
matter, were welcome and useful to Cable and Cahan—either as
possible ways out of chronic economic precariousness or simply as
the best way available for them to gain recognition. But in the very
terms of their "acceptance" can be seen a deadly misconception or
minimizing of their true concerns. That is, there are obvious
ironies—a bizarre air of unreality, actually—in imagining Cable,
the clear-eyed author of *Old Creole Days, The Grandissimes, Strange
True Stories of Louisiana, The Silent South*, and *The Negro Question*,
those five books, all written before 1890, that Edmund Wilson says
"ought to be read by every student of American literature," being
bracketed and celebrated with the sentimental Hoosier Riley.[9] Or
to see the Jewish socialist intellectual and immigrant Abraham
Cahan cheek-by-jowl with Richard Harding Davis, the swash-
buckling Anglo-Saxon bearer of the white man's burden.

The ironies and significance of Cable's career have been well-
documented in the excellent study by Professor Butcher, Professor
Turner's exemplary biography, and in Edmund Wilson's splendid

7. Quoted in Rudolf Kirk and Clara M. Kirk, "Abraham Cahan and William
Dean Howells: The Story of a Friendship," *American Jewish Historical Quarterly* 52
(Sept. 1962): 41.

8. *Literature and Life*, p. 182.

9. Edmund Wilson, "The Ordeal of George Washington Cable," *New Yorker*,
9 Nov. 1957, p. 204.

review-articles, "The Ordeal of George Washington Cable."[10] I simply want to underline their general observations. They all point in one way or another to the damage done him, first by his Southern critics—because of his strong criticism of the South's attitude toward race and his own advocacy of Negro rights (the New Orleans historian Gayarré, after the appearance of "The Freedman's Case in Equity" [1885], said "the author of *The Grandissimes* is as deprived of all moral sense as a crocodile")[11]—and then to the process by which he was worn down by Northern publishers and editors so that this talented social critic was finally converted, as Wilson says, into "a false romantic novelist." Right from the beginning, what the Northern editors had really wanted from Cable was "little love stories of queer old New Orleans—the romance and charm of the French Quarter, those Creoles with their droll English." We will see that this was not the essential Cable. By 1895 Richard Watson Gilder, editor of the *Century*, had decided the South was right in denying civil rights to Negroes and was warning Cable to "beware the fate of Tolstoy." Cable was well aware, too, that by then the cause of the freedman was for the moment largely lost: the disfranchisement of the Negro and the removal of his civil rights were largely completed in the South, and in the North the urge toward forgetting past realities could be seen in the increased prominence of the plantation tradition in literature (the works of Thomas Nelson Page had begun appearing in 1884). The final irony is that Cable himself came to accept the notion of fiction as romance and produced in 1901 his only best-seller. This work, *The Cavalier*, Wilson calls meretricious and a trite mastery of the popular formulas of the time, but Cable himself was delighted with it.[12] The sapping of his very real talent had taken place. By 1918, in his last novel, he came back to a more serious treatment of the subject of race in the South, but he never again wrote a book as good as *The Grandissimes* (1880).

What precisely was the subject and the nature of the achieve-

10. Philip Butcher, *George W. Cable* (New York: Twayne, 1962); Arlin Turner, *George Washington Cable: A Biography* (Durham, N.C.: Duke University Press, 1956); Wilson, "The Ordeal of Cable," pp. 172–216.

11. Wilson, "The Ordeal of Cable," p. 194.

12. Ibid., pp. 174, 200–201, 202, 210.

ment in *The Grandissimes*,[13] a work that Newton Arvin, Edmund Wilson, and most critics agree is Cable's best, and how is that to be reconciled with the image of him, a scant seven years after its appearance, being lionized for his ability to project "the lilt of Creole dialect"?

To be sure, there are a faithful rendering of the physical setting in New Orleans in 1803, painful attention to the sound of English rendered by the Creoles, certain sentimentalities, as in the portrait of his heroines (over whom Howells gushed); but over and above all, it seems to me, was his devastating attack upon the central assumptions of the Southern aristocratic tradition in literature, and indeed, upon the South's civilization as a whole. Cable did not flinch from his conclusion that this civilization was based on the fundamental evil of slavery and that a vicious racism had been constructed to rationalize it. Over and over again Cable makes this explicit in the novel, usually through the person of the German immigrant Frowenfeld, who functions as raisonneur, and who bears some interesting resemblances in his morality to Cable himself. Speaking of New Orleans society, he says, "here is a structure of society defective, dangerous, erected on views of human relations which the world is abandoning as false" (p. 152). "The greater part of our troubles comes from —" the hero Honoré Grandissime asks. "Slavery," answers Frowenfeld, "or rather caste" (p. 154). (By adding "caste," Cable underlines his intention to talk of his own time as well as ante-bellum days.) A long speech by Honoré, when it is observed that the horrible darkness in which the civilization sits is cast by "The shadow of the Ethiopian" capably sums up the situation as seen by Cable:

> "Ah! My-de'-seh, when I try sometimes to stand outside and look at it, I am *ama-aze* at the length, the blackness of that shadow! . . . It is the *Némésis* w'ich, instead of coming afteh, glides along by the side of this morhal, political, commercial, social mistake! It blanches, my-de'-seh, ow whole civilization! It drhags us a centurhy behind the rhes' of the world! It rhetahds and poisons everhy industrhy we

13. George W. Cable, *The Grandissimes: A Story of Creole Life*, introd. Newton Arvin (New York: Sagamore Press, 1957). All references are to this edition, and will be inserted in the text.

got! . . . It brheeds a thousan' cusses that nevva leave home but jus'flutter-h up an' rhoost, my-de'-seh, on ow *heads*; an' we nevva know it!—yes, sometimes some of us know it."

He changed the subject. [P. 156]

M. Grandissime changes the subject, as did many Southerners and Northerners—there were some subjects simply too sore to the touch, as Honoré says earlier in this same dialogue with Frowenfeld, and that he is simply "afraid to go deeply into" (p. 154). Cable's first achievement was that he was not afraid to go deeply into the subject.

His second achievement, closely allied to the first, was his ability to avoid, by and large, the stereotypes of abolitionist or plantation tradition in portraying Negroes—becoming, in Sterling Brown's authoritative judgment, "one of the finest creators of Negro character in the nineteenth century."[14] The blacks Cable portrays are of many types and are everywhere in the book, while over all hovers the story of the African Prince Bras-Coupé. To be sure, Cable helped establish the stereotype of the tragic mulatto in his portrait of Honoré Grandissime, free man of color, half-brother to the hero of the book (who has the same name). But even in this portrait, as Brown notes, Cable based himself on a greater degree of fidelity to New Orleans reality than those that came after him, and his focus on a tragic man was already more unusual than the more popular octaroon heroine.[15] Cable balances this portrait with the grim, commanding, and imperial figure of the quadroon Palmyre la Philosophe—"this woman [who] had stood all her life with dagger drawn, on the defensive against what certainly was to her an unmerciful world . . . [a woman who] by inexorable decree, . . . belonged to what we used to call 'the happiest people under the sun.' " And then Cable adds one beautiful, simple sentence that explains why, as the plantation tradition of Page and Harris grows, he will be able to achieve fame only as a quaint writer of dialect, not as the tough realist he was: "We ought to stop saying that" (p. 135). There is also his great creation of the figure of

14. *The Negro in American Fiction* (1937; rpt. ed., Port Washington, N.Y.: Kennikat Press, 1968), p. 67.

15. Ibid., p. 65.

Clemence, the shrewd folk-heroine. Clemence's wiliness, her deep and moving expression of human emotion, are of no avail against her white aristocratic tormentors—in one of the most chilling scenes imaginable, she is almost lynched, given some hope, then cold-bloodedly shot. Throughout the book there are servants, little messenger boys, figures in the field (a trite point, but worth noting, since so many depictions, and critical estimates, of American landscape omit the ubiquitous black laborer). Preeminently, however, there is the story of Bras-Coupé, that is hinted at, alluded to, led up to, as if toward an important emotional climax.

The story is that of a giant African Prince who is captured and brought into slavery. He refuses, however, to accept any notion of his own inferiority or to engage in undignified menial labor. At last, he is brought to submission when he is offered Palmyre, with whom he is smitten, as his bride. She sees in him a putative insurrectionary (a Touissant L'Overture), worth developing. At his wedding party, he drinks wine, gets drunk, smites his master, and is forced to flee for his life into the swamps. He places the plantation under a voodoo curse; and most of his guerilla ventures thrive. But then under the influence of wine again, he risks coming into public, and is captured. The rigorous Code Noir, the instrument of the master-class for dealing with rebellious slaves, is invoked. Bras-Coupé is lashed, his ears are cut off, he is hamstrung. As he lies dying, a priest asks him if he knows where he is going, and he answers simply, "To Africa." The poignancy and overtones of this story need no great elaboration.

This was the story that an editor of the *Atlantic Monthly* had rejected in 1873 because of its "unmitigatedly distressful effect," as well he might have. It is the germ of the novel, over which it broods, and toward which most of the characters direct their fascinated attention, and from whose consequences no one is entirely free. For his candid exploration of race, violence, the flaws of Southern society, Cable has justly been called the "spiritual godfather" of more recent Southern writers,[16] but I doubt that many of them, Faulkner (for the most part) included, go as directly to the heart of the issue as Cable did in his early work.

One speculates on the success of more recent Southern writers

16. *The Grandissimes*, introd., p. v.

and the reasons for it. On the one hand, those who strike the "tragic" note emphasize the violence, and are aware of race and the flawed South, but tend to associate these with a generalized "human condition" rather than the specific facts of Southern life and its peculiar institutions. On the other hand, liberal Southern novels, say *To Kill a Mockingbird* and *Intruder in the Dust*, exploit the theme in ways that are uplifting to a certain kind of white reader: in these books *true* aristocrats join forces with women or children to save the abused black from corrupted post-slavery white rabble. In this process, the misery of the blacks is simply an instrument for the moral instruction in noble individual values of the young white aristocrat (of the spirit). Both of these books, incidentally, were best-sellers. The simpler and more candid Cable, however, has to be periodically rediscovered.

ABRAHAM CAHAN

In dealing with the case of Abraham Cahan, it will be necessary to discuss briefly the role William Dean Howells played in encouraging, introducing and, in a sense, promoting Cahan. In 1892 the fiery Socialist editor of the Yiddish *Arbeiter Zeitung* and the Dean of American letters met, on Howells's initiative, so that Howells might get first-hand information about "walking delegates" (i.e., union organizers). Much to Howells's surprise, Cahan had for several years been an admirer of his work, and was quite knowledgeable on the subject of literature in general. A few years later, having by chance seen a story of Cahan's in an English-language magazine, he encouraged Cahan to complete a manuscript on life on the Jewish East Side. Howells then succeeded, after much difficulty, in getting it published as *Yekl: A Tale of the New York Ghetto* (1896). This was, so far as I know, the first full-fledged immigrant novel (i.e., by and about immigrants) in America. He then gave the book a rave review on the first page of the *New York World*'s literary section.

What was Howells's interest in all this, and what might be worth looking at, from a fresh perspective, in the Howells-Cahan friendship?[17] First of all, we must begin to see Howells's role in the late

17. This subject has been dealt with at length by the Kirks (see n. 7, above),

eighties and through the nineties somewhat more analytically than has usually been the case. The traditional picture is that after the Haymarket Affair in 1886, Howells's social awareness deepened, he turned increasingly toward social issues in his work and life, and that in the process he encouraged and welcomed many younger realists (Henry Fuller, Stephen Crane, Frank Norris, Cahan, and others) who were writing about the less "smiling aspects" of American life during this period of acute change. By and large, this portrait seems to me a true one; but it must be qualified by an awareness of Howells's ambivalences in this period. The ambivalence was well summed up in a letter to his father in 1890, when Howells described himself and Mark Twain as "theoretical socialists and practical aristocrats."[18] I think Sanford Marovitz is too harsh when he categorically indicts the so-called renaissance in Howells's social thinking in this period for being "as ephemeral as his sensitivity for the poor and the Jews was shallow."[19] Marovitz documents this "shallowness" fairly convincingly, and it is the touchstone of his judgment of Howells's sincerity, but then I think he does not go far enough when he locates the source of this superficiality in Howells's peculiar psychological make-up without analyzing the social basis of that make-up. This mistake is avoided in an earlier, invaluable study by Kermit Vanderbilt, in which the focus was upon the *social* meanings of Howells's ambivalences. In Howells's attitude toward immigrants, the poor, and Jews, for example, Vanderbilt discovers an essential contradiction in Howells: his need on the one hand, as a midwestern commoner, to champion a democratic ethos in order to justify a rise in elite Boston surroundings (anyone of talent could be embraced by the official culture), but on the other hand, the need, once one has "made it," to insist upon the superiority of the elites (which implies a disdain for other rising groups, such as the Irish and the Jews) in

---

who rely largely upon translation from the fourth volume of Abraham Cahan's five-volume autobiography, *Bletter fun Mein Leben* (New York: Forward Association, 1926–1931).

18. Sanford Marovitz, "Howells and the Ghetto: The Mystery of Misery," *Modern Fiction Studies* 16 (1970): 362.

19. Ibid., pp. 361–62.

order for the rise to be stabilized and to *mean* something.[20] Henry Nash Smith has shown, even earlier than Vanderbilt, how ambivalence toward the *official* culture, but on a deeply disguised level, was the key to understanding both Howells's and Twain's bizarre behavior in connection with the Whittier Birthday Dinner in 1877.[21]

In my view, Howells was always impelled by his contradictory impulses, and by strategies for evading their true import and consequences. His brand of realism, his politics, his very style, seem to me a compromise, an effort to minimize these conflicts in his own life. Basically, as Ziff notes, Howells "was of the establishment, yet keenly aware of its shortcomings" (p. 45). He accepted the role of spokesman of the intelligent middle class, whom he would try to educate—in one way, by encouraging other writers more at home in the era of perplexing social issues. In this period of an enlarged social awareness, Howells was essentially a mediator—just as he had been earlier in his friendship and encouragement of those two such dissimilar American writers, Mark Twain and Henry James. Howells did heroic and priceless work in using his position to introduce fresh, dissident talent to frequently indifferent or philistine audiences—and this contribution should not be minimized—but the process of mediation and accommodation therein imposed worked both ways. In this context his relations with Cahan can be better understood.

Another way to see the situation is that Howells was acting out a version of the ritual by which he became a mainspring of the high culture. Just as some New England sages knew after the Civil War that they would have to make way for some new Westerner properly respectful of the role of New England and its culture, and had adopted Howells as precisely the right man, so Howells knew that the culture he now so well represented would have to absorb some of the new elements. Quite naturally, he responded to those divergent voices that could at some essential point be accommodated to his own central assumptions. He was perfectly at home, for ex-

20. *The Achievement of William Dean Howells: A Reinterpretation* (Princeton: Princeton University Press, 1968), esp. ch. 3, pp. 96–143.
21. *Mark Twain: The Development of a Writer* (Cambridge: Harvard University Press, 1962), ch. 5, "The California Bull and the Gracious Singers," pp. 92–112.

ample, with the requirements of the "Iron Madonna" (in H. H. Boyesen's phrase), that genteel feminine reading public whom one was not supposed to offend, and his distaste for literary challenges to conventional sexual morality are well known. He could warmly receive Stephen Crane's *Maggie*, for example, but not the amoral sexuality of Dreiser's *Sister Carrie*, a sexual approach more in keeping with the new commercial age in America.

Thus, with regard to Cahan, Howells must have been favorably disposed to welcome a representative of the mysterious, swarming foreign masses—who might at first glance disturb one by his superior grasp of Russian literature and of socialist theory (Howells was then involved with both, but not in Cahan's passionate and engaged way)—when that representative revealed upon their first meeting that he had read every line Howells had written and was "an inspired reader and follower."[22] Furthermore, despite his considerable achievements away from the mainstream of American life, Cahan knew his experience was parochial, and he was properly respectful of American culture and cultivation. Here is Cahan, describing dinner at the Howells's, where he was invited to talk about his *Yekl* manuscript:

> Howells's wife and daughter were at the table. In his house everything looked aristocratic in the American manner. The scent of spiritual nobility was in the air. Mrs. Howells held herself with American graciousness, but with American tact and true hospitality.[23]

Moreover, from 1886 onward—after Haymarket and the Henry George campaign for mayor of New York, into which Cahan threw himself—Cahan's own efforts were increasingly directed toward educating and Americanizing Jews and toward broadening out the more sectarian aspects of radical politics and publishing. Paradoxically, an advocate of speaking to the masses in their own tongues, he was an avid student of English from the moment of his arrival in the United States in 1882, mastering it so quickly that by

22. Cahan, *Bletter*, vol. 4, p. 31.

23. Ibid., p. 34. The translation of this passage in the Kirk article omits the last two uses of "American" as adjectives, and gives "formality" rather than "graciousness" as the meaning of "tsierlichmannerlichkeit." I believe my restorations and revision give a rather different and important emphasis to the relationship; everywhere else I agree with the translation.

1885 he was certified to teach the language to immigrants in a New York City evening school. For many years, then and afterward (until his irrevocable commitment to the *Jewish Daily Forward* in 1903), Cahan flirted with the hope of a career in English journalism or letters.

This concern with the English language as the foremost vehicle for the transmission of cultural values must not be underestimated. We know what a powerful instrument of social and intellectual control it can be—how, for example, children of subcultural [!] minorities can be induced to internalize feelings of inferiority because of failure to conform linguistically to dominant cultural standards. The immigrant's English was a crude and ineffectual instrument, and his own language tended to be seen as valueless or contemptible, except as a transitional stage in the acquisition of the language of the dominant group or culture (if not by the immigrant generation, which might, then, have to be "sacrificed" to frightful labor and living conditions, then to his children. Or so runs, I think, the popular mythology.).

When Cahan, impatient at the stupidity of the editors who rejected *Yekl*, had it printed in Yiddish, Howells was at first distressed, but then smiled and observed, "It means that the book hasn't been published."[24] This was, to all practical intents and purposes, true. When it finally did appear in English, in 1896, the terms of Howells's glowing acceptance are worth reflecting upon: "What will be the final language spoken by the New Yorker?" he asks, in what is patently a cultural question: i.e., New York will clearly become the dominant literary center of the nation— Howells's own shift from Boston in the late eighties was a sign of that. What, then, will be its essential qualities? Really, the question might be, will it be controlled and dominated by the new immigrants? Howells touches urbanely upon the possibility:

> We shall always write and print a sort of literary English, I suppose, but with a mixture of races the spoken tongue may be a thing composite and strange beyond our present knowledge. Mr. Abraham Cahan, in his "Yekl, A Story [*sic*. It should be *Tale*] of the New York Ghetto" (Appleton's), is full of indirect suggestions upon this point. Perhaps we shall have a New York jargon which shall be to English what the

24. Kirk and Kirk, "A. Cahan and W. D. Howells," p. 37, n. 10.

native Yiddish of his characters is to Hebrew, and it will be inter-
larded with Russian, Polish and German words, as their present
jargon is with English vocables and with American slang.[25]

Some few years after this, in *The American Scene* (1905), reflecting
upon a visit to the East Side in the company of a leading Yiddish
playwright, Henry James would, in his inimitable way, draw out
the anguished implications for "high culture" in this state of affairs.
He was not able to observe it as dispassionately as Howells presumably had. According to James,

> . . . in these haunts of comparative civility we saw the mob sifted and
> strained, and the exasperation was the sharper, no doubt, because
> what the process had left most visible was just the various possibilities
> of the waiting spring of intelligence [i.e., here was no lump of people
> passively accepting notions of their intellectual inferiority because
> they had not mastered the King's English]. Such elements consti-
> tuted the germ of a "public," and it was impossible (possessed of a
> sensibility worth speaking of) to be exposed to them without feeling
> how new a thing under the sun the resulting public would be. That
> was where one's "lettered" anguish came in—in the turn of one's eye
> from face to face for some betrayal of a prehensile hook for the lin-
> guistic tradition as one had known it.[26]

James was not as sanguine as Howells—but then he did not have
before him Cahan's *Yekl*, in which Howells saw many features that
rendered his questions about the future of the culture rather rhetorical. Cahan's treatment of the immigrant problem—as largely
one of the immigrant's accommodation to American values, rather
than of his impact upon those values—was basically reassuring to
someone like Howells. He continues, in the review:

> I cannot help thinking that we have in him a writer of foreign birth
> who will do honor to American letters, as Boyesen did. He is already
> thoroughly naturalized to our point of view; he sees things with
> American eyes, and he brings in aid of his vision the far and rich per-

25. Ibid., p. 51.
26. *The American Scene* (New York: Charles Scribner's Sons, 1946), pp. 138–39.

ceptions of his Hebraic race; while he is strictly of the great and true Russian principles in literary art . . . "Yekl" is, in fact, a charming book.

Then at the very end of the review, as if in answer to the question he had posed at its beginning: "I had almost forgotten to speak of his English. In its simplicity and its purity, as the English of a man born to write Russian [*sic*. Cahan was "born to write Yiddish"] it is simply marvelous."[27] Reassured himself, Howells reassures his reader that Cahan really is "one of us"; the center holds.

Predictably enough Howells praises the language of the narrator, which completely envelops and is obviously superior in every respect to the crude, painfully rendered immigrant's English. The narrator is capable of frequent conceptual formulations "placing" the story in a wider historical context, unlike the immigrant's language that is sharply set apart from it. In a love scene, for example (chap. 8, "A Housetop Idyll"), the characters attempt to handle unfamiliar emotions with their broken English and seem only touching and a little absurd. The old language did not deal with such concepts as "love," while the new one is grasped only in clichés; the result is a sense of their acting out forces they cannot comprehend. When the characters speak in a third language, as it were, that of the native Yiddish transposed into English, there is a hint of more inner richness than their English suggests. In this, of course, lies the poignancy of the immigrant generation, a theme beautifully developed much later by Henry Roth in his 1930s classic *Call It Sleep*. None of this was picked up by Howells. The tale is that of the transformation of the immigrant Yekl to "Jake the Yankee," a process that involves his giving up his old spiritual and religious values, dress, appearance, and casting off his pious, simple old-world wife, while taking on, as Howells puts it, "our smartness and vulgarity with an instinctive fitness for that degree of fellow citizenship."[28] That something painful is going on in this Americanization process, even for someone as callow as Jake, is movingly imaged in the concluding sentences of the book:

27. Kirk and Kirk, "A. Cahan and W. D. Howells," p. 52.
28. Ibid., p. 51.

But the distance between him and the mayor's office [where Jake was going in order to marry his new wife and become thoroughly committed to the new American values] was dwindling fast. Each time the car came to a halt he wished the pause could be prolonged indefinitely; and when it resumed its progress, the violent lurch it gave was accompanied by a corresponding sensation in his heart.

It did not matter that this note in the book was not emphasized—the reading public was not especially interested in either its pathos or its charm. As the editor of *Harper's Weekly* had put it upon rejecting the tale, "the life of an East Side Jew wouldn't interest the American reader," or, as another (from *McClure's*) had said, why didn't Cahan "write about beautiful things?"[29] Howells's review made a great difference to Cahan personally in that he was immediately accepted as a serious writer, and became for a while a celebrity. But, as John Higham notes, "*Yekl* sold poorly and was soon forgotten despite Howells's promotion."[30]

Cahan wrote some short stories thereafter dealing with some of the themes adumbrated in *Yekl*, aspired briefly to a career in English letters, but then went back to Yiddish journalism in 1903, where he remained until his death in 1951. Twenty years after *Yekl*, he published the fullest development of his reflections on the ambiguities inherent in the immigrant's life in America, his classic *The Rise of David Levinsky* (1917). This book should be understood on a deep level to be about the price an individual or group pays when, for the sake of success in material terms, it temporizes with its best self. After this, unable or unwilling to proceed further along this lacerating theme—which also did not succeed at the time with a *large* American audience—Cahan stopped imaginative writing altogether. Like Howells, in one sense, he thereafter encouraged other writers during the flowering of Yiddish culture in the 1920s and 1930s.

29. Ibid., pp. 34–35.

30. *The Rise of David Levinsky* (1917; rpt. ed., New York: Harper, 1960), introd., p. ix.

CHARLES CHESNUTT

Now to a consideration of the last two "regionalists" I have chosen to talk about, partly in illustration of how misleading and damaging such a designation can be. I will, necessarily, be considerably briefer in my discussion of Charles Chesnutt and Kate Chopin.

Charles Chesnutt tended to be praised in his time and ours as a short-story writer, although with the exception of an unusually perceptive introduction to a reprint of *The Conjure Woman* (Chesnutt's first book, published in 1899, reprinted 1969),[31] little has actually been said about his stories that suggests the true nature of their meaning and achievement. More often, his novels are talked about, and then in rather extreme terms. We have either excessive praise, as when Saunders Redding, angered at Chesnutt's absence from most anthologies, called him "a far better novelist than his much better known contemporary, William Dean Howells," or the rather peremptory dismissal of Robert Bone, who considers the novels failures because of their overt propagandizing and Chesnutt's failure to master "the aesthetic requirements of the [novel] genre." Nor is this simply a case of black vs. white critic, in that Redding was anticipated in his high estimate by Russell Ames, whereas Bone's views have been echoed by Darwin Turner and LeRoi Jones.[32]

Now that the six books Chesnutt published between 1899 and 1905—two collections of tales, a biography of Douglass, and three novels—have been reissued after lying in relative obscurity for over sixty years, and given our new general interest in the black presence in America, we can hope for an assessment of Chesnutt as

31. Charles Chesnutt, *The Conjure Woman*, introd. Robert M. Farnsworth (Ann Arbor: University of Michigan Press, 1969).

32. Redding, "The Problems of the Negro Writer," in *Black and White in American Culture*, ed. Jules Chametzky and Sidney Kaplan (Amherst: University of Massachusetts Press, 1969), p. 364; Bone, *The Negro Novel in America* (1958; rpt. and rev., New Haven: Yale University Press, 1965), p. 38; Ames, "Social Realism in Charles W. Chesnutt," *Phylon* (1953): 199–206; Turner, introd. to Charles W. Chesnutt, *The House Behind the Cedars* (1900; rpt. ed., London: Collier-MacMillan Ltd., 1969), pp. vii–xx; Jones, *Home: Social Essays* (New York: Wm. Morrow and Co., 1966), pp. 105–7.

a novelist based, at the least, on wider familiarity and discussion. At the moment, I do not want to confront these novels directly, but to go back to *The Conjure Woman* and to some other uncollected stories. In them, I think we will find what was unique in Chesnutt, and learn why the hopelessness of this uniqueness being understood by the reading public of his time perhaps drove Chesnutt to those strategies in his novels that have been deplored by his detractors, and that ultimately silenced him as an imaginative writer.

In a nutshell, what Chesnutt created in his stories, within the framework of folkloristic "goopher" or conjure and transformation tales—partly in response to the stereotypes of Thomas Nelson Page's fantasies about plantation life—was the first conscious, fictional form given to the black ethos in America. My use of the term "black ethos" comes from Professor Sterling Stuckey's demonstration of the existence of such an ethos in slavery, observable, he says, in the folklore of black people. Stuckey defines this black ethos as a "life style and set of values . . . which prevented [black people] from being imprisoned altogether by the definitions which the larger society sought to impose."[33]

It is that ethos which John, the friendly, white, Northern narrator of the conjure tales *occasionally* glimpses in the stories told to him and his wife by the shrewd old ex-slave in his employ, Uncle Julius, but he is basically too obtuse, or rather too thoroughly in the grip of his own prejudices, ideology, and self-concern to fully credit or understand it.

Here is the glimpse, in an early story "Dave's Neckliss" (1889), that was unfortunately not included in *The Conjure Woman*:

> It was only now and then that we were able to study, through the medium of his recollection, the simple but intensely human inner life of slavery. His way of looking at the past seemed very strange to us; his view of certain sides of life was essentially different from ours. He never indulged in any regrets for the Arcadian joyousness and irresponsibility which was a somewhat popular conception of slavery; his had not been the lot of the petted house-servant, but that of the toiling field hand.[34]

33. "Through the Prism of Folklore: The Black Ethos in Slavery," in Chametzky and Kaplan, *Black and White in American Culture*, p. 173.
34. Charles W. Chesnutt, "Dave's Neckliss," *Atlantic Monthly* 64 (1889): 501.

But then almost at once the narrator's bland complacency, and blindness, intrudes when he reflects on what he conceives to be the "shackles" on the mind of Uncle Julius:

> Whether the sacred name of liberty ever set his soul aglow with a generous fire; whether he had more than the most elementary ideas of love, friendship, patriotism, religion,—things which are half, and the better half, of life to us; whether he even realized, except in a vague, uncertain way, his own degradation, I do not know. I fear not; and if not, then centuries of repression had borne their legitimate fruit.[35]

This kind of condescending rumination by the narrator is sometimes thought to reflect Chesnutt's own views or to be a strategy for disarming the Northern white reader. That is, by seeming to have his sentiments echoed, the reader would not be alienated, and the burden of Chesnutt's message could be obliquely presented to him. I don't think either strategy is really at work, but rather the simpler one of an ironic undercutting of the narrator and the shackles on *his* and the reader's minds. This strategy seems to me everywhere in evidence in the conjure tales, but it seems to be one fairly consistently overlooked, perhaps because the reader is too close to John's assumptions. Can we not see the wryness that must have developed in Chesnutt as his deepest ironies were ignored or misconceived? If the conjure stories reveal anything, they reveal that Uncle Julius—and behind him black people generally—have a much more than "elementary" grasp of the ideas of love, friendship, patriotism (if we mean by that love of the *best* ideals of one's country), and religion. They reveal, in fact, the rather superficial grasp of these concepts by the white John.

John knows that there is usually a personal interest served by each of Julius's tales, and he is willing to wink at that—it is a motive he benignly understands—but invariably he limits their true import by regarding them as merely amusing or only fanciful. His wife, Miss Anne, her mind not bound as her husband's is by business and practical concerns and the superficial "rationality" geared to their execution, is better able to feel and understand the human

35. Ibid.

essence at the heart of the black man's experience. But John's limited sympathy, his inability to fathom Julius's experience, Robert Farnsworth concludes in his fine introduction, "is a hauntingly familiar projection of the white response to America's racial problem."[36]

It is generally thought that emboldened by the success of his early stories (usually for the wrong reasons), Chesnutt moved out into more direct attacks on racism. One might argue, instead, that Chesnutt rather despaired of his audience examining his work closely enough to get at its substance rather than its surface. Given the urgency of the problem, he would move to the attack in a more accessible way. But his work was launched against the tide, in whatever form it came: from the heart of the black ethos (and therefore oblique and sophisticated to the uninitiated) or from within the crude terms of discourse adopted from popular white literature. When LeRoi Jones laments, therefore, that the "embarrassing and inverted paternalism of Charles Chesnutt and his 'refined Afro-American' heroes are far cries from the richness and profundity of the blues," he is talking about the surface his novels had to assume, and misses entirely the unsounded depths in Chesnutt's conjure stories.[37]

A final word. In 1904, a year before his last novel, Chesnutt published a story called "Baxter's Procrustes," a "little satire" on book collectors—all white—that Bliss Perry, in accepting for the *Atlantic Monthly*, called "an ingenious and amusing story, extremely well told."[38] It is all of that—a small gem, I would say—but again, a white editor fails to see its true import. In this story, an exclusive club of collectors, the Bodleian(!), is the victim of a hoax. One of their members, Baxter, has reluctantly agreed to publish in a fine and limited edition an epic poem (which no one had seen), that is then sold to the others. The poem, entitled "Procrustes," is solemnly praised by the literary committee (who had, in fact, never unsealed their copies, or gone beyond admiring the cover

36. Chesnutt, *Conjure Woman*, p. ix.
37. Jones, *Home*, p. 106.
38. "Baxter's Procrustes," *Atlantic Monthly* 92 (1904): 823–30; Helen M. Chesnutt, *Charles Waddell Chesnutt: Pioneer of the Color Line* (Chapel Hill: University of North Carolina Press, 1952), p. 208.

and its type, the binding, and the apparent quality of its uncut pages). Much to their chagrin, an outsider (an Englishman), hearing the high praise, opens a sealed copy of the book only to find, of course, that the pages are perfectly empty. The cream of the jest comes in the final twist: after their initial anger, when many of the members disgustedly discarded their copies of the apparently worthless monstrosity, the president of the club points out to them that the remaining copies are now more valuable than ever:

> His Procrustes, from the collector's point of view, is entirely logical, and might be considered as the acme of bookmaking. To the true collector, a book is a work of art, of which the contents are no more important than the words of an opera. Fine binding is a desideratum, and, for its cost, that of the Procrustes could not be improved upon. The paper is above criticism. The true collector loves wide margins, and the Procrustes, being all margin, merely touches the vanishing point of the perspective.

One might be permitted to think that this little satire on book collectors makes a wry and covert comment on the literary establishment generally. Chesnutt's book the next year, *The Colonel's Dream*, an attack on the convict labor system, did not fare as well as his earlier ones, except in England, where, his daughter and biographer says, "They were surprised that the conditions depicted still existed in the South and, *having no sense of responsibility for such conditions* [my italics], gave the book much praise."[39] Chesnutt lived for many years after this book appeared (he died in 1932)—a rich, full, useful life—but he did not write anymore. Perhaps in these times we will be able to free ourselves sufficiently to read not only his letters, but—paraphrasing an old black folk-saying—his meaning as well.

KATE CHOPIN

The same, of course, can be said about Kate Chopin, with whom I conclude this catalogue of the misapplication of the term "regionalist" to several important and long-ignored writers, whose best

39. Ibid., p. 212.

work went to the heart of a changing America's dilemmas. At first admired for her stories about Louisiana, Mrs. Chopin was condemned for the candor and subject of the last book she wrote, *The Awakening* (1899).[40] She was quite unprepared for the devastating reception accorded her story about awakening sensuality and passion in a married middle-class woman who takes a lover, is briefly liberated to a new view of herself and her life, but is ultimately unable to see it through, and drowns herself. Stunned by the criticism, Mrs. Chopin stopped writing, after a decade of work that promised the development of a unique and perhaps major American talent. Her reputation and works were almost completely forgotten until she was rediscovered, only yesterday it would seem, by Edmund Wilson and Per Seyersted. To Professor Seyersted we are much indebted for collecting her work in two volumes and for an indispensable biography—both published in 1969.[41]

The condemnation, in its time, of *The Awakening* as shocking and immoral does not surprise us now, when we reflect on the reception given *Sister Carrie* only a year later because of its presumedly amoral attitude toward departures from genteel standards of sexual propriety. What does surprise one is the modernity, in numerous small and large ways, of Mrs. Chopin's insights into "the woman question." It is not so much that she advocates women's libidinal freedom or celebrates the force of the body's prerogatives—our post-Freudian age has won those battles (or should have). Nor is she terribly explicit about the mechanics of sex, in the contemporary way. What Kate Chopin shows so beautifully are the pressures working against woman's true awakening to her condition, and what that condition is.

From the opening images of a parrot in its cage (p. 1) and the marriage ring on the woman's finger (p. 5), to the final images that flash before the drowning heroine—clanging spurs of a cavalry officer and "the hum of bees, and the musky odor of pinks"

40. Kate Chopin, *The Awakening* (1899; rpt. ed., Ann Arbor: University Microfilms, 1962). All references in the text are to this edition.

41. Per Seyersted, ed., *The Complete Works of Kate Chopin*, 2 vols. (Baton Rouge: Louisiana State University Press, 1969); and *Kate Chopin: A Critical Biography* (Baton Rouge: Louisiana State University Press, and Oslo: Universitetsforloget, 1969).

(p. 303)—the struggle is for the woman to free herself from being an object or possession defined in her functions, or owned, by others. Despite her middle-class advantages—money and the freedom to pursue a talent—Edna Pontellier, the heroine, is finally unable to overcome by herself the strength of the social and religious conventions and the biological mystique that entrap her.

Along the way, nevertheless, she is vouchsafed a glimpse of life as an autonomous self. She knows the joy of being able to say she would "never again belong to another than myself" (p. 208). Her young children, however, present a great problem. She says that she might die for her children, but would not give up her essential selfhood for them (pp. 121–22). This sentiment seems admirable but it is somewhat ambiguous, for at the end, in a muddled way, it is precisely the image of the children and her uncertainty about the nature of her role toward them that prove her undoing. Unconcerned herself about her new, freer attitude toward illicit sex, she fears the effects it will have upon her children when they learn about it. Mrs. Chopin had shown earlier how the husband uses the children and the mother's presumed duties toward them as a means of control and subjugation of the woman, but she is, finally, at a loss as to how to break through to newer and more humane conventions—a legitimate and recognizable dilemma. More startling to contemporaries must have been Edna's sentiments after her fall into adultery, and with a most unworthy lover. Whatever the conflicting emotions that assail her, she says, "there was neither shame nor remorse" (p. 219).

Edna's struggle toward a new state of awareness and independent being is to some extent understood and encouraged by only one other woman in the book—the pianist Mme. Reisz. But this strange woman's encouragement takes the form of urging a kind of self-sufficiency that is as selfless as the marriage vows: if Edna is serious about her work as an artist, then she must give herself to it entirely—a renunciation, really, of the flesh and conventional human relationships. That, of course, is an answer, but no answer to the woman's question posed in this book: how to be free in one's self and for one's self but still meaningfully connected to others. Posed in this way, the question, of course, applies to everyone. What makes it peculiarly related to the woman question in *The Awakening* is Mrs. Chopin's unwillingness to make her heroine's situation easier by removing from her selfness the burden and possibility of motherhood. As indicated earlier, Mrs. Chopin stumbles ambiguously on this question, as indeed we still do.

Awakened by a realization of her sensuous self, Edna Pontellier grows in self-awareness and autonomy. But it is a lonely and isolated autonomy that exacts a terrible price. Like Kate Chopin herself, who broke through to new perceptions and honesty as an artist, Mrs. Pontellier, in the context of her time and milieu, found no firm ground beneath her, either in theory or practice, and she went under.

SUMMARY AND CONCLUSION

This brief study of the work, reception, and fate of four so-called regionalists whose most significant work and concerns were misunderstood or unappreciated in their time might lead us to several related conclusions:

1. That the kind of regional or local-color literature most appreciated at the end of the nineteenth century by white middle-class audiences and critics would not be likely to probe too deeply or obviously into social problems that characterized the emergent modern America. Such problems as the roots and consequences of ingrained racism, ethnic upheaval, and immigrant acculturation, unconventional codes of personal behavior and morality suggested real challenges to the dominant eth-class's[42] notion of a culturally homogeneous nation. These were, precisely, the problems dealt with by Cable, Cahan, Chesnutt, and Chopin, which might help explain their poor reception.

2. That the descendants (in a certain sense) of Cable and Cahan—Southern and Jewish writers—in our time seem largely to have been accommodated to the core culture, perhaps because in the forties and fifties they lost or gave up (with a few exceptions) some of the fundamentally critical potentialities or perspectives in the work of their predecessors. The descendants of Chesnutt and Chopin, on the other hand, have only more recently emerged to challenge the augmented center. It may well be that the black chal-

---

42. Milton M. Gordon's useful category, discussed in *Assimilation in American Life* (New York: Oxford University Press, 1964).

lenge will be more uncompromising than the earlier challenges, while women are only at the beginning of an assault whose full dimensions remain to be seen.

3. Finally, and most obviously, I think we may see once again how literary work and literary evaluation are ineluctably, if sometimes obscurely, influenced and illuminated by the times and the cultural currents in which they are produced.

Two

The Assimilation of the American Jewish Writer:

Abraham Cahan to Saul Bellow

The starting point for these observations is the appearance of two publications at the end of the 1950s. On 6 November 1959, the *Times Literary Supplement* was devoted to "The American Imagination," a sequel to *TLS*'s first special supplement on American literature five years earlier. The 1959 issue included a long article on a subject not previously mentioned: "A Vocal Group—The Jewish Part in American Letters." The year before, Mr. Leslie Fiedler delivered three important and provocative lectures surveying what he called, martially enough, "the break-through" of the American Jewish writer.[1] These lectures were collected in 1959 and published as a pamphlet entitled *The Jew in the American Novel* (New York: Herzl Institute Pamphlet 10, 1959).

Two things should be said at once about both the *TLS* piece and Mr. Fiedler's articles. First, the number and quality of the writers discussed in them provide impressive evidence, by any standards, of the important part played in the American literary scene by writers of Jewish background. Second, there is the awareness that it was in the 1950s that this part became most apparent and most significant. Before this time of course there had been American writers of Jewish background, but it was only then that a difference in the quality of their contribution to American letters

1. In a long article based on these lectures entitled "The Breakthrough: The American Jewish Novelist and the Fictional Image of the Jew," *Midstream* 4, 1 (Winter 1958), 15–35.

became apparent. What was discerned is that many serious writers turned toward the materials of Jewish life in America without an awkward self-consciousness that had led in the past to a crippling defensiveness, sentimentality, or hatred.

A persuasive explanation of the changes apparent in the writing of American Jewish writers over three generations is that by the 1950s, the Jewish situation itself had changed in America. By then the Jews had moved well beyond the stage of cultural trauma familiar to all new immigrants, or of the aggressive-defensiveness of the *arriviste* making his way in an essentially strange, if not actively hostile, society. By the 1950s a secure Americanism seems to have been won—a position, at the least, of nonmarginality. A growth in the idea of tolerance in America, following upon the frightful example of the horrors to which intolerance could lead in Nazi Germany, undoubtedly played a part (as Oscar Handlin has pointed out),[2] as did effective Jewish "defense" and cultural organizations operating within a favorable social and political climate. Among writers and intellectuals, the process of acculturation, after several decades of immersion in American life, had taken place more quickly and firmly.

I will briefly illustrate this process of acculturation over three generations in the work of several writers. The process may be seen as a kind of assimilation into the broader stream of American letters. I use the term "assimilation" provocatively: it must be understood within a specifically American context, whose meaning will be suggested throughout this paper. Primarily, I am concerned to show what "assimilation" means to the American writer of Jewish background as *writer*—that is, through an analysis of language, what differences of tone, point-of-view, and meaning are revealed in the characteristic work of writers of three generations.

II

Let us consider some examples in the work of several Jewish writers representing these generations. The work of Abraham Cahan, Michael Gold, Clifford Odets, and Saul Bellow exempli-

2. *Race and Nationality in American Life* (New York: Doubleday, 1957), p. 145.

fies three stages in an evolution toward the assurance, poise, and wealth of linguistic and emotional resources that are the precondition of important literary creation. My illustrations fall into two groups, each revealing three ways in which a common subject is treated.

The common element in the first group of three examples is the speaker's attempt to convey an emotional attitude toward his mother. Such a situation inevitably tests a writer's ability to project sentiment without sentimentality and emotion without hysteria—in short, the extent of his control of his materials and expression:

> 1. As I went to bed on the synagogue bench, however, instead of in my old bunk at what had been my home, the fact that my mother was dead and would never be alive again smote me with crushing violence. It was as though I had just discovered it. I shall never forget that terrible night.

> 2. My humble funny little East Side mother. . . . She would have stolen or killed for us. . . . Mother! Momma! I am still bound to you by the cords of birth. . . . I must remain faithful to the poor because I cannot be faithless to you.

> 3. Mamma surrendered powers to her that maybe she had never known she had and took her punishment in drudgery; occupied a place, I suppose, among women conquered by a superior force of love, like those women whom Zeus got the better of in animal form and who next had to take cover from his furious wife. Not that I can see my big, gentle, dilapidated, scrubbing, and lugging mother as a fugitive from such classy wrath, or our father as a marble-legged Olympian. . . . But she does have a place among such women by the deeper right of continual payment.

The first excerpt is from *The Rise of David Levinsky,* by Abraham Cahan. Published in book form in 1917, *Levinsky* is sometimes thought to be the classic, if not the greatest, novel of the Jewish immigrant experience in America.[3] Cahan was editor for many

3. See James D. Hart, *The Oxford Companion to American Literature* (New York, 1956), p. 109, in which it is reported that the novel has been called "America's greatest Yiddish novel." Leslie Fiedler concurs in the high estimate of the book, although he considers its real subject to be "loneliness" (*The Jew in the American*

years of the *Jewish Daily Forward*, America's most widely read Yiddish-language newspaper. Cahan came to the United States from Russia in 1882, the year the great migratory waves began, at the age of twenty-two. He was a prolific writer, almost always in Yiddish, although in the 1890s he was writing for several important English-language newspapers, and was even, for a time, the American correspondent for Russian newspapers. He died at the age of ninety-one, having been an important and influential figure in American Jewish affairs throughout his long life.[4]

The narrator in the novel looks back upon his life from the vantage point of a successful garment manufacturer of sixty. As a boy, he was a Yeshiva student in a Russian *shtetl;* at seventeen he migrated to the United States. He develops new patterns of thought in the desperate business of making a life in America, takes pride in such achievements as the acquisition of a new language, and of business success, but is disappointed by certain emotional failures. This scheme of the book provides Cahan with a good vehicle for much realistic observation, especially of such relatively exotic matters (exotic to his contemporary American audience) as life on the old East Side of New York and the ins and outs of New York's important new garment industry. But the discrepancy Levinsky feels between his past and his present status—the two halves of his life do not "comport" well, he says—adds a poignancy and depth to the novel that transcend its purely sociological interest. What Cahan has caught and fixed—and I think unconsciously, for his intention was not consciously ironic—was a reflection of the discrepancy in the very language and mode of thought available to Levinsky—and behind him Cahan—and the experience it is meant to render and express.

> As I went to bed on the synagogue bench, however, instead of in my old bunk at what had been my home, the fact that my mother was

Novel). For a strong dissenting view on the novel, see Morris U. Schappes, "Anatomy of 'David Levinsky,' " *Jewish Life* (August 1954): 22–24. The phrase "Yiddish novel," incidentally, is misleading. The book was written in English, originally for serialization in *McClure's Magazine*, where it appeared in 1913 as "An Autobiography of an American Jew."

4. Moses Rischin, *The Promised City, New York's Jews, 1870–1914* (Cambridge, Mass., 1962), pp. 124–27.

dead and would never be alive again smote me with crushing violence. It was as though I had just discovered it. I shall never forget
that terrible night.

Levinsky is trying to convey a sense of tremendous loss. What
emerges, instead, is a *report* that a loss has occurred. The emotional impact of the passage is stifled by the language; indeed, it
is never really released because of the language. The passage is
"correct," but lifelessly stiff ("the fact that," "It was as though I had
just . . ."), literary in the worst sense of that word ("smote me with
crushing violence," "that terrible night"), above all *described*, as if
from the outside. We are *told* that he was "crushed," and that the
night was memorably "terrible"; there is no dramatization of these
emotions. If this first passage is incapable, finally, of transmitting
a fully dramatized sense of loss, it is probably because the loss was
too great and traumatizing. It was too much part of a world irrecoverably lost, yet unassimilable, to the writer, especially in
a language newly mastered.

The next passage is from Michael Gold's *Jews without Money*,
published in 1930. It was widely read at one time (going through
eleven editions in its first year) in the original and in many transla-
tions. Gold was editor at the time of *New Masses*, and his book
strongly influenced the style of the short-lived (1930–1935) vogue
of proletarian fiction. Gold belongs to a second generation of
American Jews. The book chronicles, more or less connectedly, in
a series of presumably autobiographical sketches, the hard life of
thousands of impoverished Jews living on the East Side of New
York during the early years of the century. The passage cited attempts to convey the nostalgic affection and commitment to his
past that is the basis of the narrator's firm commitment to the poor.
It is a step forward, we see, from Levinsky and the sense of the
irrecoverable quality of the past and the hollow sense, therefore, of
loss of both past and future.

> My humble funny little East Side mother. . . . She would have
> stolen or killed for us. . . . Mother! Momma! I am still bound to you
> by the cords of birth. . . . I must remain faithful to the poor because
> I cannot be faithless to you.

The final commitment ("I must remain faithful to the poor . . ."), I submit, is less than convincing in the context, because the initial commitment sounds to our ears so mawkish. The three adjectives, "humble," "funny," "little," are being asked to carry a large burden of emotion and sag a little, with a dying fall, under the weight.[5] These lines express, too, how *far* he's come from his mother (and past) and how separate he considers her from him, to be able to refer to her—surely with unconscious condescension—as "humble, funny, little." This adds an element of strain and a certain forced quality to his *assertion* (and that is all it can be) that he'll "remain true."

And yet, there is a strong, even violent, emotion evident in the passage, "She would have stolen and killed for us." Levinsky would never have permitted himself this revelation in such blunt terms. There are two voices jostling for dominance in this passage—and an inability, finally, to integrate them or to decide between them. "Mother!" and "Momma!" side by side—two worlds—which is it to be? If the narrator really is umbilically bound to the past, can he really be as complacent as the bravado tone suggests? Surely the rhetoric sounds forced and overdramatized? That these questions can arise reveals the uncertainties, the tensions, that exist in this second, or transitional, phase.

And so we come to the third excerpt: from Saul Bellow's *The Adventures of Augie March*, published in 1953. Bellow, one of the most distinguished contemporary novelists, may be thought of, from one point of view, as a peculiar product of the American intelligentsia—which sets him apart at once from such familiar and hallowed names as Steinbeck, Wolfe, Hemingway, and Faulkner. He has long been a teacher in the universities, but more to the point, his thought took shape in the avant-garde of literature and politics, and in the magazines of that avant-garde. *Augie March* is Bellow's celebration of experience; explicitly, his celebration of the American experience. His two earlier books had been introspective, thoughtful parables influenced by, among others, Dos-

5. Fiedler amusingly and accurately characterizes the sentiment in this passage when he says that Gold "can also sing 'A Yiddishe Mamme' in a proletarian version." *The Jew in the American Novel*, p. 31.

toevsky; *Augie March* was different in tone and style, and was the first book to win wide attention—it was awarded the National Book Award in 1953.[6]

To the subject he celebrates, his form—a sprawling, episodic, apparently picaresque novel—seems peculiarly appropriate: as if that sprawl and shapelessness is America. But the formlessness is superficial and deceptive. The novel has a tough center, a consistent line of development, in the character of Augie March. His fate (which, he informs us in the opening sentence, quoting Heraclitus, is *character*) is inextricably bound up with his experience, but, paradoxically, transcends it. Augie searches through and beyond his experience toward the essential: his own identity, that most elusive commodity, which slips away from his grasp in the very act of grabbing. As a novel centering on the quest for identity, it is as securely in the American grain as are the novels about Ishmael and Huck Finn. Augie March, fatherless, without a firm past and code to live by, embodies an important theme running through the fictional image of the American experience. He is also Jewish and from Chicago, and the experiences he has would be recognizable to other urban Jews of his generation.

> Mamma surrendered powers to her that maybe she had never known she had and took her punishment in drudgery; occupied a place, I suppose, among women conquered by a superior force of love, like those women whom Zeus got the better of in animal form and who next had to take cover from his furious wife. Not that I can see my big, gentle, dilapidated, scrubbing, and lugging mother as a fugitive from such classy wrath, or our father as a marble-legged Olympian. . . . But she does have a place among such women by the deeper right of continual payment.

There is authority behind Bellow's language—assurance and precision in his thought and emotion. He is unapologetic in beginning the passage with "Mamma!" He knows who she is, and more important, who he is. No cloying sentimentality is attached, nor

6. From this perspective, it might almost be seen as the literary fulfillment of the American intellectuals' "return to America" announced, urged, and marked by *Partisan Review*'s 1952 symposium on "America and the Intellectuals."

any fear of overvaluation—or nasty Oedipal overtones—when he elevates her with a simile to the world of the Greek gods. One resource that saves the passage from pretension, mere rhetoric, or sentimentality, is Bellow's sure use of the ironic, deflating energy of the vernacular (as in the expressions, "a fugitive from such classy wrath," "a marble-legged Olympian"). Where Gold's mother was "humble" and "little," Bellow's is "big" and "gentle"—so far the same: "purr" words as Stuart Chase might say. But Bellow's soft adjectives are immediately made palatable by his use of the vigorous, visual, and certainly deflating "dilapidated" and "lugging," to complete the series. The combination of learning and observation, of high style and vernacular, by its wit and delicate irony convinces us that here is an author *in control*. The voice of this "I" is free of inhibitions, his mind free of preconceptions, it is the voice of a narrator at ease with himself. He has placed his mother accurately. Distanced and mythicized—as a consort of a god she is not to be patronized from a distance as "humble, funny, little"—she is nevertheless present and solid and humble as life. The final sentence, therefore, can convince us of the narrator's unambivalent affection for her memory.

III

The second group of selections—"The New World"—again reveals the pattern I have discussed above. The first and third are again the words of David Levinsky and Augie March, while the second is an excerpt from Clifford Odets's *Awake and Sing*, from 1935. It serves the same purpose as the excerpt from Gold's book—Odets, too, being of that radically minded generation of the early thirties. Odets is probably the best playwright produced by any American left-wing theatre of that period.

1. The immigrant's arrival in his new home is like a second birth to him. . . . I conjure up the gorgeousness of the spectacle as it appeared to me on that clear June morning: the magnificent verdure of Staten Island, the tender blue of sea and sky, the dignified bustle of passing craft—above all, those floating, squatting, multitudinously windowed palaces which I subsequently learned to call ferries.

2. JAKE: From *L'Africana* . . . a big explorer comes on a new land—"O Paradiso." From act four this piece. Caruso stands on the ship and looks on a Utopia. You hear? "Oh paradise! Oh paradise on earth! Oh blue sky, oh fragrant air—" MOE: Ask him does he see any oranges?

3. I drank coffee and looked out into the brilliant first morning of the year. There was a Greek church in the next street of which the onion dome stood in the snow-polished and purified blue, cross and crown together, the united powers of earth and heaven, snow in all the clefts, a snow like the sand of sugar. I passed over the church too and rested only on the great profound blue. The days have not changed, though the times have. The sailors who first saw America, that sweet sight, when the belly of the ocean brought them, didn't see more beautiful color than this.

Again, in the first example we perceive language that seems to come to the writer second hand. It is high-sounding and scrupulously literary: "I conjure up," "magnificent verdure," "tender blue," "dignified bustle"—and diction that is painfully pretentious: if Levinsky has learned to call "multitudinously [and where have we seen that word outside of *Macbeth*?] windowed palaces" "ferries," he apparently has not learned to call "verdure" trees and grass, nor a "spectacle" anything but "gorgeous."

He opens the passage by describing the immigrant's arrival as a second birth—and indeed it is and must have been—but bemused by those ferries, where is the pain and glory and wonder of birth? The older Levinsky is really caught by the contrast between what he is and has become with that other, "green" Levinsky, who thought that ferries were palaces, so that the experience of rebirth is sidetracked completely. In this passage, there is not only a failure of communication, as in the earlier Levinsky passage cited, but a failure of the narrator to fix exactly what it was he was trying to communicate.

Odets's dialogue is from *Awake and Sing*, his first and, with *Waiting for Lefty*, his best-known play. The action of the play centers on a Jewish family hammering out their lives in a Bronx apartment, whose confining quality is made even more oppressive by the bleak depression period in which they live. The first speaker, Jake, the idealistic grandfather, is a retired barber who tries to retain his dignity while forced to live off his children. He is an immigrant, who retains humanistic and socialistic ideals in an Old World, bookish way. One of his last functions, as he sees it, is to impart to an embattled grandson some of his ideals—as well as the material and spiritual means to free himself from sordid surroundings. This speech communicates well his loftiness of vision, his aspiring nature, his faith that Utopia can be seen, can be achieved, here and now, and its scene is the New Land. Moe, the second speaker, is a one-legged veteran of the First World War who makes his living as a "bookie." Moe Axelrod is the real hero of the play: American-born, he is tougher, more cynical (on the surface) than old Jake—and more in touch with the vernacular realities of American life. His "ask him does he see any oranges?" is a perfect, ironic deflation of Jake's impassioned, but self-deluded vision. In his reply is to be seen the same undercutting of the naive immigrant as in Cahan's piece, but more subtly done, and Moe's discomfort is a more honest expression of the uneasiness Gold displayed in his "Mother! Mamma!" passage. And yet Moe and Jake like each other. Jake's vision and his expression of it are, after all, felt along the bone and expressed honestly: the phrase "a big explorer comes on a new land" is unpretentiously in Jake's own language, the foreigner's English, and he lets the blue sky speak for itself.

The two views, the two voices, neither penetrate nor wholly invalidate the other, finally, but there is no synthesis—as perhaps there need not be in a dramatic situation. They merely exist, side by side—the old and the new, the past and the present, the lofty promise of America and the hard-boiled lessons learned in its streets. This excerpt dramatizes well, I think, the bifurcation of sensibility in the second, transitional generation of American Jewish writers.

And so, again, to Saul Bellow's *Augie March*. Augie has been in anguish most of the night before the scene here described. He was with a friend in the labor room of a hospital while she lost a baby and, for reasons too complicated to summarize, has had his engagement to an attractive, rich young girl broken off as a consequence. On this New Year's Day, then, we are also in the presence of a rebirth—one life has ended for Augie and another is about to begin as he looks out upon a new land.

When Bellow talks of the "profound blue," is it only my ear that

detects a personal resonance in the adjective "profound," instead of
the cliché I detect in Levinsky's "tender?" In any case, Augie sees
a "sight," not a "spectacle." Further, when the mother ocean gives
birth to the new-world traveler, it does so, Augie unself-consciously asserts, from its "belly." And surely the double comparison
compounded of homely materials—not to mention the alliterative
grace—of "a snow like the sand of sugar" is simply beyond the
linguistic resource of Levinsky. The homely materials—the vernacular, if you will—comport well with learning ("cross and
crown together, the united powers of earth and heaven") and an
aspiring ideal. One frame of reference does not contradict another:
both are aspects of an enlarged and confident sensibility. The "I"
starts quietly and simply in this passage—over a cup of coffee—
and carries us with assurance—with no sense that we are being
"had"—to an affirmation that the promise of America still exists
and is valid.

Our navigator here styles himself "a Columbus of the near-at-
hand." Behind him, Saul Bellow, of course, is the real explorer of
the new territory. For, as Fiedler has observed, with Bellow in the
early 1950s, we approach the period of the Jewish writer's liberation from his material. This sounds paradoxical. What I mean,
simply, is that the writer is now free to bend the materials of his
experience to his independent vision. He can approach those materials without shame, uneasiness, or uncertainty. The inability to
do this, in one degree or another, comes through, I believe, in the
work of Cahan, Gold, and Odets. One way of seeing this is to think
of Cahan as saying, in effect, "I can write English as well as the
Gentiles," whereas Gold and Odets, at a later stage, seem to suggest that this doesn't matter at all—so long as the emotion is
honest—and *their* struggle was to find the honest emotion. With
Bellow, however, these problems seem simply to drop away. The
language he uses is unquestionably his and, his present being
secure, he can regard the past with a clear eye.

In the period ushered in by Saul Bellow—one of acceptance and
achievement (a kind of assimilation) in the world of letters—the
writer could use whatever he wished of the Jewish past or Jewish
present in America. This could be done without obsessiveness or
without a sense of wounds suffered from his experience as a Jew.

When "Jewishness" is seen to be a factor among serious Jewish writers of the fifties, it will often be so from the vantage point of, and with the aim of accommodating it to, a secure Americanism. In the process, one senses, also, with the wide differences among such writers as Saul Bellow, Bernard Malamud, Philip Roth, Delmore Schwartz, Karl Shapiro—to name only a few—the drive to discover, name, win back (or perhaps only not to lose) some important part of themselves.

This last impulse may not be as paradoxically related to "a secure Americanism" as it first seems. First of all, while the opportunity for this fresh exploration of self arises from a secure position, the *impulse* to do so may also have come as a reaction to a certain bland, characterless image of American society from which so many intellectuals recoiled in the gray-flannel-suited Eisenhower years. The opportunity and the impulse do work together—to the enrichment of both the specific, peculiar self and the wider society. In an article on Bellow written at the end of the fifties, J. C. Levenson sums up this development exceedingly well:

> The Negro, the Catholic, and the Jew have in the present generation joined the Southerner in discovering the advantage of being in a conscious minority; if the politicians and authors of textbooks had not been saying so for so long, one might speculate that this is one of the most viable ways to be an American.[7]

What this means, I must make clear, is that acculturation—or assimilation as I have used the term—in an American context does not have to mean faceless conformity to a conforming society, but rather the reverse: to the discovery of the resources and human richness inherent in differences. The assimilated American writer (that is, the American writer) does not have to placate an Establishment, real or imaginary. He does not have to write like T. S. Eliot, a Southern agrarian, or a Presbyterian elder—although he is of course free to do so and will achieve an audience if he is good enough—but he is free also to write about, discover, and celebrate life seen from his own vantage point.

7. "Bellow's Dangling Men," *Critique* 3, 3 (Summer 1960): 11.

Three

Immigrant Fiction as Cultural Mediation

The concept of mediation in my title may be taken in several ways, although I start with a conception deriving from the Frankfurt School of Critical Theorists' use of the term. They were concerned to address and correct the old base-superstructure dichotomy in classic—some would say simplistic—versions of Marxist thought, in which culture and consciousness are regarded as reflections of a social, economic, historical base—Marx's "real foundation." This reflective theory of consciousness—which has not been limited to Marxists, of course—and its products (literature and art chief among them) has the effect ultimately of burying cultural artifacts in their contexts, which makes it impossible to justify or understand the uniqueness of literature and art. These ideas have been frequently and adequately refuted numerous times in the past—I do not want to rake over old coals. But I do want to establish my basic thesis and the ground for it. That is, consciousness and its products are integral and constitutive elements of "reality," not mere reflections of some other more basic, primary reality. They are the essential means by which human beings live, by which they know and shape what their experience is all about. Human culture is the creation of forms and modes (of behavior, ritualizing, representing) that enable people to grasp, give meaning to, and get through their lives.

A paper presented at MLA, 29 December 1981, as part of a panel on "Jewish Immigrant Fiction: A Retrospective View."

In the course of their interaction, immigrant and American culture produced such various forms and modes in profusion. It is a vast subject. Fortunately, on this occasion the emphasis is on fiction alone, and on Jewish immigrant fiction (and, I would add, the descendants of immigrants' fiction). One can hope to begin to deal with that. And I will take seriously the overall intention of this panel, which is to provide a retrospective view, but also move along in time to the descendants of immigrants.

The exploration of this literature's function as mediator and creator of culture, a meaningful way of being in the world, should start at an obvious starting point: with the first book by "The Father of World of Our Fathers." Abraham Cahan's *Yekl: A Tale of the New York Ghetto*, published in 1896, was perhaps the first novel in English wholly about the immigrant experience—or at least of this period of the so-called second immigration, the great one that began in the 1880s—and the first by an immigrant writer.

In his indispensable essay on "Literature and Ethnicity" in the *Harvard Encyclopedia of American Ethnic Groups* (1980), Werner Sollors has a marvelous paragraph—one that also starts with *Yekl*—on rooftop settings in Jewish-American writing:

> In Cahan's *Yekl*, for example [he writes], the "housetop idyll" [chapter 8 of the novel] is more than an incidental "realistic" setting for immigrant Jake's incipient alliance with the more Americanized Mamie Fein; . . . this scene is a symbolic battle between Old World past and the New World future, and the sheets [flapping on a clothes line] are consciously metamorphosed into the shrouds of Jake's father and the covers of Mamie's bed. [Interestingly, there is a rooftop scene in the movie version, "Hester Street," but none of this is in it. As I will explain later, the film is for us, now, and incorporates and creates other meanings appropriate for its assumed contemporary audience. Sollers continues:] In Zangwill's *Melting Pot* (1906) the final scene takes place on the tenement rooftop to allow the cosmic dimensions of the American symphony full play against the red skies of the Fourth of July and with a full view of the Statue of Liberty [the symphony is a key symbol used later by Horace Kallen in his influential work on cultural pluralism] . . . The rooftop functions as Mount Sinai. Even in Gold's *Jews Without Money* the rooftop is the place of metaphoric

closeness to the Old World, where the narrator's father tells Romanian folk tales. And in Roth's *Call It Sleep* the rooftop is the locus of a Joycean epiphany, a revelation of complexity.

Few readers [Sollers concludes] attempt to read ethnic literature as evidence for the existence of rooftops; but the example of what even "realistic" or "socially oriented" writers do with so simple a motif serves as a warning against reading imaginative literature as social evidence. [P. 663]

In short, one need not read Jewish immigrant fiction to know that there were tenements and that they had flat roofs on which immigrants spent time, or that there were hallways and cellars and stoops and pushcarts. And mothers and fathers, present or absent. However, the choices made of *what* to include and what not to— what needed to be dealt with, as it were—are of course crucial and do provide a kind of social evidence, if of a special kind.

The key to the kind of social evidence provided is the kind of reader implied by the text. Crudely put, whom it presumably addressed (I say presumably, because so often it is of course the writer himself or herself that is the implied reader), and then why, and to what purpose. To answer these questions, attentive reading of the text, not empirical studies of a readership, is the best method.

First, the literature helps to familiarize the strange artifacts of life encountered in the immigrant experience—the opposite of Brechtian *entfremdung*, although that also takes place (I am thinking of certain religious and traditional figures in Cahan's short stories). A good example of the kind of estranging and distancing technique occurs, if I may be allowed to move away from fiction, in the film version of *Yekl*. At the end of "Hester Street" is the wonderful *get* scene (the divorce between Jake and Gitl), in which the great Yiddish actor Zvi Schooler magically transforms the shabby situation and setting (the high point of the script by Joan Micklin Silver) by solemnly intoning in Yiddish what the divorce contract states. The sentence I am thinking about is the one which locates them all geographically, wherein the mundane East and Hudson rivers (between which this city of New York is located) become timeless rivers that could have been the Tigris and Euphrates, indeed, any of the habitations in which Jews have found themselves in their millennial history. In a single stroke, we perceive the strangeness, as it were, of American Jewish life, or rather, its character as yet one more episode in the history of the people, rather than an all-embracing and final reality.

That scene and that awareness did not occur, or at least not in this fashion, eighty or so years earlier in Cahan's novel. A contemporary audience needs perhaps to be jolted into this kind of awareness—the same kind of thing Philip Roth achieves in his early story, "Eli the Fanatic." In the midst of affluence and a presumably secure Americanism, one needs to be reminded of where we came from, who we are, the burden of our history. For Cahan and his generation I would surmise that such an awareness was never far from the surface, was a given, and the task of someone like Cahan could seem to be that of domesticating and familiarizing the immigrant to the strange new world. Thus Yekl/Jake is recalled quickly to his familial duty when he hears of the death of his father early in the book; a solemn moment. But in that scene on the rooftop in chapter 8, after the superficiality of his efforts to accommodate that past to his present American reality is all too clear, the memory of the father and those old world values are recalled in the flapping of bedsheets—and that whole ethos threatens to collapse into pathos or burlesque. Yekl is a rather sad and callow figure.

But then for whom was Cahan writing? It is easy to say for a non-Jewish audience—for *them*, the middle-class Americans—the *goyim*. In *Yekl*, there is of course internal evidence for that: the footnotes explaining Yiddish terms, the set-piece essayistic chunks in the book on the character of the lower East Side and the various Jewish populations there. And external evidence as well—Howells's invitation to Cahan to write the book (for him and his public as it were), and his efforts to get it published, and in a sense to be reassured about their superiority to these strange immigrants. But remember a little-known fact of the book's appearance: when Howells could not easily place the manuscript with a publisher, Cahan grew impatient and began to print it serially in Yiddish in the *Forward*. So it was, in Cahan's view, at least, kosher for *that* audience as well. Incidentally, at this occasion—a panel sponsored by the American Association of Professors of Yiddish—

it is worth recalling, wryly, that when Howells found out what Cahan was doing, he was at first dismayed, but then he reasoned that publishing in Yiddish wasn't really publishing, and shouldn't interfere with his efforts to get it properly and respectably published (which he subsequently did). The same kind of thing may be said for *The Rise of David Levinsky*, Cahan's masterpiece and one of the best immigrant novels ever written. Obviously it was written for *them*: *McClure's* commissioned it originally and it was printed there in four installments in 1913 as a means of informing the great American public about the exotic Jews and their business success. Interestingly, by the third and fourth installment, *McClure's* began to introduce, quite misleadingly if one read only the text, (in my view) anti-Semitic illustrations, summaries, and captions. That is a story in itself, which I will not go into now.

That was certainly not what Cahan was about, nor the novel. Much of it was precisely the accommodating and legitimating of a unique and strange experience. Thus an immigrant audience is shown dressing American, summer resorting, speculating in real estate, building a great industry (the garment industry), as well as dealing with such new situations as boarders, love affairs, linguistic and political nuances in generational conflicts, loneliness. I am proposing that the audience was a Yiddish one (or at least an immigrant one) as well as the obvious Yankee one. When James Hart, in his *Oxford Companion to American Literature*, called it "the greatest Yiddish novel"—although it was conceived and written in English, and only much later translated for serialization into Yiddish, he was in error, but he was right, too. I suppose the immigrant novel of this generation performed a function similar to the traditional one always cited about the origins of the English novel—as supplying the English middle class with instruction and legitimation as it rose to prominence. However, it must be said that the *great* vehicle for the immigrant's socialization into American culture was probably the early motion picture—so much a product of immigrant entrepreneurial abilities and the needs of a public shaped by that experience, as well as others affected by urbanization and industrialization generally. Think of early Chaplin and other films in that way, as vehicles for accommodating this new public to the technological and cultural artifacts of the day—telephones, office machines, trolleys and flivvers, not to mention tenement apartments, sinks and stoves, dance halls, restaurants, leisure time activities. It all did go on in fiction as well—although the singularity of the fiction, or at least of the work by Cahan I am familiar with and have cited, is that in addition to all that, Cahan was basically *meditating* on the meaning of it all, for himself and others in his curious cultural situation. He tried to put together the phenomenon of biculturality, trying to see if the two parts of his life might fit together. Levinsky concludes at the end of his narrative that they do not comport well—and so the feeling of fragmentation and cultural unease we are left with. That is a profound theme. Cahan was no Tolstoy or Chekhov, although he was strongly influenced by and tried to emulate them (in fact, it is possible that Cahan's ideal implied reader was Russian). Cahan's achievement was to let us sense the shifting sands beneath an apparently hard and real surface of life.

Beyond this aspect of familiarizing the strange in the immigrant novel is the second phase or process of accommodation: mythicizing the artifacts and crucial relationships of the new cultural situation, and sometimes sentimentalizing, romanticizing, or trivializing them. For example, the Yiddishe Momma, patiently patting her *latkes* and *lukschenkigel*—or whatever—while clucking worriedly over her son, urging him to "eat, eat" is *not* a truth of nature. I am not even sure it was a significant historical reality—though it has become in time a powerful social and sometimes sociocomic myth. Jules Zanger has an important article on how the Jewish mother theme began and developed through three stages.[1] First, at the turn of the century (and continuing, of course), the tender and loving mother who could turn fierce as a wolf to protect her family from external threats; then the switch, which he locates in Odets's Bessie Berger in *Awake and Sing*, wherein the ferocity is turned against the family; thus setting the stage for the Bitch Mother of Bruce Jay Friedman and the presumably obnoxious Sophie Portnoy. It is a rich and exemplary essay, abounding in insights about the social and psychological conflicts being worked out or represented in these various treatments. I want to add a few notes, modifying some things, underscoring others.

First, it should be said that none of these types or stereotypes

1. Jules Zanger, "On Not Making It in America," *American Studies* (1977): 39–48.

appear in Cahan's work, although Levinsky's mother does turn fiercely on hooligans who had attacked David, and she dies for it. Rather than her being taken as an example of the fierce wolf-mother, however, I am interested that Cahan kills her off, as it were, back in the home country (it all happens in Russia), where he also leaves fathers (in *Levinsky* and in *Yekl*). Cahan's work abounds in Jewish women, and not a sentimentalized figure among them: they work, dance, think (or don't), read (or don't), act, do, love, renounce—in short are figures in their own right, neither to be condescended to nor mythicized.

Perhaps the sentimentalization develops in vaudeville, through the twenties; perhaps as Zanger cogently observes, it becomes a way that Americanizing sons can expiate a certain guilt. Thus we have the conclusion of Gold's *Jews Without Money* (1930), which I analyzed earlier:

> My humble funny little East Side mother. . . . She would have stolen or killed for us. . . . Mother! Momma! I am still bound to you by the cords of birth. . . . I must remain faithful to the poor because I cannot be faithless to you.

This mother/momma appears throughout the depression years in one version or another. She must be removed from the scene. Bellow tries to effectively desentimentalize her in *Augie March*, as I have shown, by putting some classical distance between him, her, and the audience. In the early fifties, Bellow was in effect announcing a more secure hold on the literary as well as the social situation.

I first wrote about the passage in *Augie March* more than twenty years ago, and upon rereading it for this occasion, I find myself still resonating to it. It moves me, I suppose, because I came of age intellectually with Bellow on my shoulder, although the slightly younger Philip Roth also speaks to and for me in quite different style.

Bellow injected the energy of the vernacular and his knowledge of the high style—his ease with high culture—to desentimentalize the mother. But he is still mythicizing her. Disclaiming the classical associations, he nevertheless relies on them to get over any emotional problem she or her previous representations might evoke. He avoids social or Oedipal stickiness with his cool control of it all. But the deep emotional resonance of the material and its previous exploitation and sentimental debasement required stronger medicine. I believe Philip Roth provided it with his portrait of Sophie in *Portnoy's Complaint*. Unlike Bellow, who found it easier to deal with Grandmas, Roth plunges in, or plunges the knife in, deep. In doing so he kills off the Yiddishe Momma or the How To Be a Jewish Mother routine (Dan Greenberg's title), joke, myth, slur, canard, once and for all; and good riddance.

That is not a universally shared view of Roth's achievement, but surely an audience of Yiddish professors knows that Yiddish literature has so often been a literature of satire and critique, and not seldom of its own community and mythicized shibboleths. Having said that, let me recapitulate the kind of social evidence one can garner from reading these texts for their implied readers.

Cahan was mediating between the *goyim* and the old Forward Association—although for each he had a separate persona when operating with their separate languages. In English, he taught *them* that *we* are not so bad, even when we *are* bad. (Yekl is a boor, for example, and Levinsky, a hollow man, certainly not a danger to anyone but themselves.) And he taught us that the world out there was real, sometimes strange, but real and negotiable, albeit not always happily.

The next generation—Odets, Gold, Sidney Kingsley in *Dead End* (I find myself drawn to the plays of the depression era, a time when the triumphs of vernacular that would make a Bellow and a Roth possible were hammered out)—were caught between Mother and Momma, were writing for us and themselves, and forget *them* (the *goyim*). That was the discovery and liberation of the depression generation, though an embattled and uncertain one. When they do address the others, the *goyim*, as in a way *Dead End* does, it is with the message that Attention Must Be Paid (Arthur Miller, of course, is the last of that group, finishing off the thirties in the late forties). The social message is a throwback, however, to Jacob Riis's *How the Other Half Lives*, and hasn't much changed in most social protest literature since. You will remember that Riis concluded his 1890 expose of bad living conditions with an image of "The Man with a Knife." If you don't give him better housing, and so on, look out, he'll get you! The perennial theme, appealing to *their* self-interest. That is about as much as *they* get into it. Mainly, as I have said, it is for us, this literature of the second-generation immigrant son or daughter of the thirties, legitimating our lives and streets. When I saw *Dead End* as a kid in Williamsburg, I remember the jolt at realizing that I lived in a slum! My first response was to be alarmed in ways I had never thought to be, but the deeper response was a kind of pleasure. We were in the movies: not bad. We were certainly not outside of the human experience of our times. We were even being flattered into thinking it was *the* human experience, the important one, of our time.

The third generation—or those of us who grew up through the forties and began to read Bellow in the fifties—felt that here indeed, with absolute authority, someone was also writing for us. But we were insiders now, we were all Augie Marches who could handle the Harvard five-foot shelf *and* the lessons of the streets, achieving the kind of urban intensity and brilliance we learned and taught others to value. What had happened, of course, was a new *social* move and a new literary position, even dominance.

Finally, with Roth the ethnic and immigrant trip seems to me done and gone. Done to a fare-thee-well—certainly for the second-generation ethnicity, about which Deborah Dash Moore writes so perceptively.[2] Roth does that scene as well as anyone ever has or likely will. No longer having to write about slums, Roth is the chronicler of second-generation neighborhoods. His Jersey City background is the urban neighborhood drenched, as Moore says, "with ethnic dimensions" (p. 388), that stands for all of the others like it in the Bronx and Brooklyn. Finally, in Roth's recent work, the *neighborhood* is also *over*. The last scene of *Zuckerman Unbound* concludes on precisely that note. The neighborhood has reverted back to a slum, but occupied by others—blacks, of course—for whom *we* are the *them*.

The problems of split personae, split experience and personalities, the luxuries of sentiment and righteousness, or of literary and classical distancing, seem over—or at least clearly inappropriate in

2. Deborah Dash Moore, "Defining American Jewish Ethnicity," *Prospects* 6 (1981): 387–409.

the present. Zuckerman seems to be saying goodbye to all that, for which his dying father's last word to him is, "Bastard!"

If there were time, one should do more with fathers—dying and dead, killing and killed—in Jewish fiction to complement the Jewish mother theme I noted briefly. One should also do fathers and daughters, starting with the intensity of Anzia Yezierska's *Bread-Givers*. And daughters and mothers.

But now we are talking about the son of a tradition—and bastard or not, Zuckerman seems to me at last contemporary with himself, poised to enter history without illusion, speaking only for himself and for writing. It will be interesting to see if it is not already too late for that.

II

History, Myth, and the
Ethnic Question

Four

History in I. B. Singer's Novels

The novels specifically under consideration are *The Family Moskat* (New York, 1950; reissued 1965) and *The Manor* (New York, 1967). The first is a complex weaving together of the fortunes of scores of Polish Jews whose lives touch those of the Moskat family from around 1900 to 1939. Until the First World War and its aftermath, the presence and spirit of the irascible, powerful, and wealthy patriarch Meshulam Moskat presides as the unifying center of this large, Warsaw-based family. After his death the disintegrative forces of that time and place, and within the family, forcefully display themselves. The story ends with the family and the larger Jewish community of which it is a part at the brink of destruction by the Germans. The second novel deals with a slightly earlier period. It begins in 1863, the date of a failed Polish insurrection against Russia, the point at which Poland began its emergence as an industrial nation, and concludes at the end of the nineteenth century. It too centers largely on the fortunes of a family, that of Calman Jacoby, a pious, honest Jew who prospers in this period by responding sensitively to the new direction of events. Part One ends with Calman in despair over his no longer simple life. Although rich, he considers his situation—with a deceitful wife, an apostate daughter, envious and malicious neighbors—a living hell; he is in retreat from the modern secular world.

Both novels, as can be guessed from even this cursory summary, display many similarities in method, tone, point of view and, on a deeper level, philosophy. It is quite proper to consider them together, and to consider them separately from his other novels. Broad in scope, epic in their intention to trace historical movements and the destiny of a whole people over the course of many decades, uncomplicatedly realistic, even-handed and steady in the writing, they seem to stand apart from *Satan in Goray*, *The Slave*, and *The Magician of Lublin*.

As I have argued elsewhere (*The Nation*, 30 October 1967), however, there are important connections among all his works, so that even the most dissimilar reveal the constant presence of Singer's peculiarly dualistic sensibility. His dedication of *The Family Moskat* to his older brother I. J. Singer should be applied even more to himself: "a modern man [with] all the great qualities of our pious ancestors." That is, significant themes and, more important, Singer's attitude toward his material (the "matter," after all—whatever the form of the fable or narrative—is, fundamentally, a concern with the meaning of human life) can be shown to be repeated and essentially unchanged from work to work. What I have to say will, I hope, bear upon the questions of history and myth that are central to my concern with Singer's novels.

II

Satan in Goray seems to me to be in part a study of demonology: it does show quite plausibly how the process of possession of various souls by diabolical forces works. The scene is the small town of Goray in the aftermath of the Chmielnicki massacres of 1648, and the effects upon the town of the hysteria induced by hopes that the legendary Sabbatai Zevi was the Messiah. Actually, the focal point of the book is the opposition of images of order and disorder. An old rabbi, Benish, leaves the disorder of Lublin for the calm of Goray, there to help establish an orderly life for himself and the surviving remnant of Jews based on a strict but not unkind observance of the traditional Law. God-Father-Rabbi in the quintessentially Hebraic dispensation is an assurance of an orderly and harmonious life. In a simple structural plan, the book first displays and celebrates this order, then shows the downfall of Rabbi Benish and the assumption of power over the town's life by the zealots, messianics, and mad sowers of discord.

It is a frightening and wholly convincing presentation, based upon an historically accurate portrayal of folk customs, traditions, and actualities. Singer is not to be seen as of the party of demonism—I suppose that goes without saying—nor, and this does require saying, is he necessarily of the party of the traditional order. His concern is to present within the framework of Jewish experience—perhaps within that experience above all others because it transcends the normal categories of history (about which more later)—the perennial struggle between order and chaos.

The same concern is evident in *The Slave*, that superbly articulated love story between a pious (but profoundly questioning) Jew sold as a slave after the Chmielnicki massacres and a Polish peasant girl (Wanda) whose family he serves. After deliverance from bondage by the Jewish community, he goes back for Wanda, whom he converts and marries secretly in defiance of both communities. Despite the hardships she must now endure, the contrast for Wanda (now become Sarah) between a life of near animality as the wife of a drunken Polish peasant and the light and grace into which she is brought as a Jew ("the image of a lady" as she sits in prayer among the other women) is near miraculous.

Ultimately Joseph, the central character, comes to a resolution and way of life that eludes Rabbi Benish and many of the other venerable sages in Singer's work. He believes, finally, that the inner spirit of the Law is more important than outward observances, holding in contempt those Jews who meticulously observe the fine points of ritual while in their personal relations displaying only small-mindedness, meanness, and self-interest. Yet, and this is important, he does not abandon ritualistic observances, at least not in the course of the book's action. For a while, we are told expositorially, after the loss of Sarah and his expulsion from Poland, Joseph believed in the false Messiah and the "unnatural" practices encouraged by some of Zevi's followers, but at the end he has come away from that sort of total abandonment. Just as the observances of traditional Jewishness saved him morally in the days of his captivity, when he lived, slept, and ate literally among the beasts, so he returns to them at the end as a necessary (but not the only or even the essential) element of an ordered existence.

This return is paralleled in *The Magician of Lublin*, another novel that is not strictly speaking "historical," but that is, like the historical novels, thoroughly grounded in a given historical circumstance. The time and setting are closer to our time, its central character Yasha Mazur as modern as any existential hero. The story is at once a parable of the artist and of modern man—amoral, skeptical, playing at God—whose end is more than likely lechery, death, despair. All of Yasha the Magician's finely spun plans, all his formidable skill, wit, and charisma, collapse into disaster. It is, from one perspective, a cautionary tale about a life lived outside traditional values and codes. In the book's epilogue, Yasha renounces the world and goes back to the old ways (and his pious wife). He devotes his days to prayers, penance, and meditation and is widely regarded, despite his disclaiming the role, as sage and rabbi, Reb Jacob the Penitent.

Now, does all of this mean that Singer is advocating a return to orthodoxy as the cure for our malaise, the void of nothingness—the chaos that preceded God's order—that yawns beneath us and before us at every moment, now and forever? In the best Talmudic fashion, we can say on the one hand yes, on the other no; but, basically, I think not. What I have suggested earlier is that Singer offers us a bodying forth in Jewish terms of the ancient and scarcely to be resolved conflict endemic to human existence. The rabbis *always* struggle against discord and disorder in themselves and in the community. Those islands of light, order, and harmony (very heaven as Calman Jacoby calls them, in contrast to the hell of modern secular existence) of the study hall, the synagogue, the rabbi's table are only momentary stays against Satan: clean, well-lighted places in a universe of *nada*. Singer is too sophisticated to believe they are anything but an image of order, just as the dybbuks of Goray are images of disorder. In *Goray*, for example, Singer is careful as narrator to distance himself from belief in the miraculous and supernatural, very much as Hawthorne, when "mingling the marvelous" in *The Scarlet Letter*, takes care to ascribe reports of miraculous occurrences to someone other than the narrator. In short, what Singer is concerned with is myth and myth-making.

Is Singer, then, essentially an ahistorical novelist? In a sense, yes, insofar as all novelists, finally, are concerned with creating or shaping stories that give coherence and meaning to the facts of life, copulation and death, and to the emotions associated with them. But in another sense, no (and here the Talmudic dialectic is helpful). Singer's great ability at myth-making is formidably authenticated by the painstaking fidelity of his mythic elements to concrete historical events, to Jewish actualities and life. The powerhouse of history, to use Philip Rahv's provocative phrase, is not necessarily and always at war with timeless myth, at least not in the work of Singer set more within a medieval than a modern world. In his novels of a concentrated and somewhat static focus, historical events provide the ground against which persistent aspects of human experience play themselves out. Singer's Jewish perspective equips him admirably for this vision of life. It is a vision that is sorely tried, however, by recent history.

III

History is movement and change. But throughout most of European history, or parallel with it, a basically unchanging footnote, the Jew, has been carried along. Professor Toynbee has called the Jewish people a fossil, a term with unfortunate negative connotations (the term and the notion have been strikingly repudiated by Maurice Samuel and others), which nevertheless points to a useful idea: Jewish survival defies history—its very existence is, in effect, mythic. Preeminently the People of the Book, or of the Law, Jews have been the bearers of an absolute through all the vicissitudes of change. Except to feel, peripherally, their effects, what did Jews have to do with the rise and fall of princes, the movements of armies and peoples, diplomatic intrigues and embassies, the stuff, in short, of "history?" Their concern has traditionally been with the relationship of man and God, of a people and God. Such a view prevailed basically unchallenged among the mass of Jews until the post-Enlightenment phase of the life of the Jewish people. At that point, the powerhouse and the myth began to collide, and it is with that collision and its effects that *The Family Moskat* and *The Manor* concern themselves.

By the middle of the nineteenth century, the bulk of the world's Jews, who were Eastern European, were beginning to be caught up in the swift currents of ideological and economic change that transformed all of Europe in that century. An almost hermetically sealed world was irreparably torn open. Liberalism, socialism, nationalism, positivism, evolutionary theory, all the heady ideas of the age made inroads upon the intellectual segments of the Jewish world. In the twentieth century, with the accelerating effects of war, revolutions, emigration, and rapid communications, the interplay of Jewish and modern life seemed complete. The process, Singer shows, was irreversible once begun. The Jews appeared to be entering, after millennia, the mainstream of European history. In the event, it proved, as we know, an illusion—a deadly illusion. At the least, the price to be paid was the traditional Jewish identity, at the worst, the German final solution of expunging Jewish existence.

There is then a certain grim logic, but one that appeals to the emotions rather than the intellect, to the Zionist and orthodox religious positions. In entering history (as Europeans or Westerners), the Jews are in danger of losing their identity as Jews. In its own way, each camp represents the position that the separateness and specialness of this people, their myth about themselves, must be maintained. Each position is essentially unhistorical. Singer's work is beautifully poised between the attractions of an ordering myth and the unsettling rush of historical realities.

In these *romans fleuves*, the older images of order persist, types and modes of thought and action recur frequently, echoing from book to book. But they become increasingly less relevant as meaningful alternatives. The kind of piety and order that solace Calman Jacoby or Moshe Gabriel of the Moskat family profoundly irritate such modern, and sympathetically portrayed men as Ezriel in *The Manor*, the skeptical rabbi's son who abandons the *capote* for medicine, or Asa Heshel Bannet, the most interesting character in *The Family Moskat*. Asa Heshel is a God-seeker and intellectual whose soul-sickness and despair at the meaninglessness of modern existence are meant to parallel the spiritual condition of Polish Jewry. Asa Heshel is literally involved in great events: he refuses to avoid the army in the First World War, he goes through the Russian Revolution, the subsequent pogroms and civil war, he is immersed in the "mainstream," the momentous events of his era. The net effect is to leave him more at sea than ever; it has all been bizarre, after all, and strangely illusory. What, finally, *does* a Jew have to do with all that? Rejected and rejecting, he is much like Joseph in *The Slave*, with a Jewish identity despite all; but unable to embrace Zionism, orthodoxy, or the complete historicism of communism, what is left for him to do, in God's name, but to die? Singer suggests that there will be a saving remnant, to be sure, in Israel, America, and Russia, but not Asa Heshel, that peculiar, proud, and doomed flower of two thousand years of Diaspora.

The last words of *The Family Moskat* draw a line under the final collapse of the messianic hope that threads its way through the Jewish faith in all of Singer's novels: "Death is the messiah. That's the real truth." In light of the Holocaust, Singer seems to be saying that all values, modern and traditional, any image of order snatched from the chaos of life, are unavailing and illusory. But one's experience of these books is by no means so negative or pessimistic. If that is so, what is the secret and the measure of Singer's achievement?

His great achievement, as a Polish Jew and Yiddish writer in our time, is not to be paralyzed by the horrors of history, or be rendered impotent by filial pieties, or become tendentious and overtly moralistic. Avoiding these pitfalls, he honorably performs his function as a chronicler, epic namer, and celebrant of well-lived and worthy lives. There are in these books astonishing images of vitality of character, place, and emotion, so that while one feels the burden of sadness in realizing that this life was annihilated, one also feels wonder and pleasure that it was truly lived, felt, real. Indeed, this is always the effect of good biography or history: mingled sadness and awe at the spectacle of the transitoriness of human life and institutions along with the astonishing persistence of recognizable human motive, desire, and aspiration. "Histories make men wise," said Francis Bacon, and in this sense, balancing between images of order and chaos, the worlds of past and present, myths and realities, the historical novelist at his best and wisest dignifies for us the pathos of human existence.

Five

Edward Dahlberg: The Jewish
Orphan in America

Perhaps it is time to stop thinking of Edward Dahlberg as the sport of American letters, whose principal achievement would appear to be his unique style. When critics today talk about Dahlberg's style, they are usually referring to his late work, his early work more often than not being regarded as a phase he had to outgrow in order to achieve his maturity. This mature style reveals itself to best effect in *Because I Was Flesh* (New Directions, 1964) in a prose that is a-dazzle with rich metaphor, erudite allusions to religious and pagan mythologies, and passionate attention to the rhythms and music of his periods. To his admirers, such as Allen Tate, Dahlberg's "formal elegance" is a vital part of his achievement (I quote from the dust jacket); to others, less enchanted, this style can often seem pretentious, arbitrary, freakish—especially when it is in the service of dubious prophecy (as in *Reasons of the Heart*, Horizon Press, 1966) and not, as in *Because I Was Flesh*, a necessary illumination of a vividly concrete center.[1] What I am concerned to state, or at least to suggest, in the short compass of this essay is that Dahlberg's mature style is a strategy for distancing himself from, and yet paradoxically possessing, the myth of his life, and that this

1. Dennis Donaghue, *New York Review of Books* 7, 6 (20 October 1966): 26–27. (Review of *Reasons of the Heart*.)

is an endeavor he shares with, say, Walt Whitman, Augie March, and scores, at least, of other American writers and Ishmaels. The first task, therefore, is to place Dahlberg securely in the American grain; the second is to assess "the myth of his life" and evaluate its relevance and force as literature.[2]

As a necessary beginning in this enterprise, I propose to look more closely than is usual at his first two books, *Bottom Dogs* and *From Flushing to Calvary*, both in their aspects as integral works in themselves and as the vital ground against which the widely recognized achievement of *Because I Was Flesh* must be measured.[3]

Much of the slang in *Bottom Dogs* (e.g., "Those micks were surefire slingers, no spiffin'," p. 73) dates the book, threatens to trivialize it, but finally can be endured by any sympathetic reader. More significantly, much of it is written in the "rough, bleak idiom" that Dahlberg decries in his preface to the reissue of the book:

> The rocks . . . rested in the diphtheria stream, like some dirty raincloud. He went around the pond, an old rotten raft on it, slugging against the mud like wet, floating rats. [P. 96]

> The alley clotted with mud, night and the spud cans of grease from Peck's Quick Lunch was spread out like a broken spider web. [P. 134]

It can be seen how this aspect, the loathsomeness of this world, is in that "naturalistic" tradition everywhere evident in American letters between *Maggie* and *Last Exit to Brooklyn*. The rats, mud, grease, and spiders of the bottom-dog world seem to have been spewed up by that same "explosion in a cesspool" so disgustedly

2. Allen Tate set the problem, and challenge, with his usual fine precision: "Criticism as we write it at present has no place for it [Dahlberg's work] and this means that I shall probably not be able to do justice to my own admiration. Mr. Dahlberg eludes his contemporaries; he may have to wait for understanding until the historians of the next generation can place him historically." "A Great Stylist: The Prophet as Critic," *Sewanee Review* 69 (1961): 314–17.

3. *Bottom Dogs* was completed in 1928 and was published in 1930 (Simon and Schuster) with an introduction by D. H. Lawrence, written in 1929. All references in this paper are to the paperback edition (City Lights Books, 1961). All references to *From Flushing to Calvary* are to the original edition (Harcourt, Brace and Company, 1932).

characterized by Paul Elmer More when he contemplated *Manhattan Transfer* a few years earlier. The naturalistic impulse, so strong in the thirties, was by no means its exclusive possession. Nor was the use of "the rude vernacular," so much favored by early proletarian realists. Dahlberg notes in his preface that he shared with other writers of the twenties (he mentions John Hermann and Robert McAlmon) the notion that they "could not write about the Midwest, Texas, or Montana except in the rude American vernacular" (p. iii). Dahlberg's free use of "the rude American vernacular," combined with his predilection for the harsh bottom-dog world of America that he had experienced first hand, suggests immediately his important position on the very eve of the depression and the subsequent vogue of proletarian realism and naturalism.[4] It is more difficult to assess fully the influence of Dahlberg upon that vogue than it is, say, that of Mike Gold, whose influence through the example of *Jews Without Money* and his exhortations in the pages of the *New Masses* is manifest. But Dahlberg's language of disgust, his imagery of rot and decay and—most important—his pioneering exploration of the bottom-dog milieux of flophouses (p. 187), hobo jungles, and freight cars (pp. 191, 198) certainly places him in the vanguard of that school.[5] In his first two novels Dahlberg charted in original fashion the territory that was to become painfully familiar in so much of the radical literature of the thirties.

There is no gainsaying this side of Dahlberg's early work—and if that were all, then he would merit, at best, a footnote to our literary history. But that is not all: what remains to be seen, and demonstrated, is the special quality of his voice and concerns.

What may strike a contemporary reader at once is the uncertainty of the narrative voice. There is inconsistency, for example, in the spelling and use of the slang, and the narrator falls in and out

4. For a first-rate discussion of how these predispositions underlay the posturing of many advocates of the new proletarian realists, from 1928 on, see Daniel Aaron, *Writers on the Left* (New York, 1961), pp. 208–12.

5. Three years after *B.D.* and one year after *Flushing*, Edwin Seaver was exhorting aspiring literary critics to go to many of those very places that Dahlberg has written about, to discover where "the strongest elements in our new literature are likely to come from." Aaron, *Writers on the Left*, p. 261.

of the bottom-dog idiom rather erratically[6]—a reflection, surely, of the author's uncertainty about his point of view toward the material at hand. And that, of course, is the crucial issue: what is he to make of the lives of his chief protagonists, Lorry and Lizzie Lewis?

These intertwined lives, this life, is the subject of his early fictions—which he more frankly calls autobiography in *Because I Was Flesh*—and it is, even in outline, an eccentric one. In *Bottom Dogs* we learn that Lizzie Lewis is the proprietor of the Star Lady Barbershop in Kansas City during the early years of the century. Lorry is her son, his paternity in doubt, who is sent off to an orphanage in Cleveland (at the behest of one of his mother's suitors) and subsequently kicks about the country in an aimless way, winding up at the Los Angeles YMCA in the company of other aimless types. In *Flushing* the story centers on the last days of Lizzie. Lorry has persuaded her to move in with him in New York, where she tries to piece together a life as an eligible "widow," renter of flats, part-time homeopathic abortionist. There are important flashbacks to Lizzie's Kansas City barbershop days and to Lorry's experiences at the J.O.A. (we learn that the Cleveland orphanage was officially the Jewish Orphan Asylum). Except for these flashbacks and one brief trip by Lorry (riding the freights, of course) back to the site of the orphanage, the entire action converges upon the moving climax of Lizzie's last operation and her death.

The elements of the life are bizarre, marginal—an almost calculated study in alienation and displacement. A lady barber? A Jewish lady barber in the heartland of America in the "Teddy Roosevelt Days" (as the first chapter in the saga is called)? A Jewish illegitimate nonorphan orphan? What indeed to make of this matter, and how to come to terms with it? That is Dahlberg's subject in the early days, and if the voice is occasionally uncertain, we should realize that he was pioneering territory only fully claimed in the fifties—chiefly in the wake of Saul Bellow's Augie March, that other Jewish illegitimate nonorphan orphan from the American heartland. Augie, however, could unself-consciously proclaim his

6. For a full discussion of this aspect of the book, see Robert A. Whitelaw, "Style in the Early and Late Works of Edward Dahlberg" (M.A. diss., University of Massachusetts, 1965).

American identity in his opening words, whereas, to Dahlberg, Lorry's life must have seemed merely eccentric. In Dahlberg's early efforts to come to grips with his subject it is too easy to see only despair or, as D. H. Lawrence says, "the last word in repulsive consciousness" (p. xvii). But this is only to see Dahlberg wearing his mask as the child of sorrows and to overlook his ambivalence: the sadness and the joy in this work, and the effort he makes to embrace both aspects in an appropriate style.[7]

In his introduction to *Bottom Dogs*, Lawrence distinguishes Dahlberg from the true tragedian who "dramatizes his defeat and is in love with himself in his defeated role. But . . . Lorry Lewis is in too deep a state of revulsion to dramatize himself" (p. xv). As usual, Lawrence's insight calls attention to something of great importance, in this case to the curious *passivity* of Lorry Lewis throughout *Bottom Dogs* and to an almost equal extent in *Flushing*. It is not true, however, as Lawrence suggests, that this condition results from mere revulsion. Certainly the rats, mud, and grease imagery, the sordid image of a world of sleazy rooms in which someone's hand is always up a woman's dress (p. 134), record the deep revulsion of the narrator toward much of Lorry's milieu. Yet much of the book reveals a narrator as elegiac as he is repulsed. The legendary figures of the orphanage, to whom he devotes chapters of his book, are after all nobodies, engaged only in petty food pilfering or desperate efforts to indulge their individuality; or the high jinks at the Y flatten out to a species of locker-room horseplay; and the culmination of the book at Solomon's danceplace, at which a young couple is married in a jazz wedding to the tune of "Avalon" (after which "the house howled, and made for the cloakrooms and lavatories," p. 266) may seem only the epitome of fatuousness and emptiness. Yet there is a stubborn sense in which none of this is just "the last word in repulsive consciousness." In the first place, much of it is funny, in a zany way reminiscent of other writers inside the whale, such as Henry Miller and Maxwell Bodenheim, and of the Beats and the black humorists. More to the point, in the orphanage sections, in the section of Los Angeles, and under the

7. Ihab Hassan does note the "savage joy" in these early books in "The Sorrows of Edward Dahlberg," *Massachusetts Review* 5, 3 (Spring 1964): 457–61.

Eighth Street viaduct in Kansas City, one is struck by the narrator's effort simply to name, and perhaps thereby claim, the elements of his experience. By the act of recording, he hopes to invest them with a kind of epic dignity, conscious always of a pathos and continuous irony in this effort deriving from their commonplace and unheroic nature. But the effort to include and legitimize and even celebrate these ingredients of what we are less embarrassed than formerly to call "an American life" seems to me to require recognition. This side of *Bottom Dogs* may best be seen in the portrayal of Lizzie—usually, as in this passage, in her own idiom:

> Well, if God would help her, perhaps she could still sell the shop, take it easier, and become a real-estate agent, do a little speculating. It was no use, you could only make so much with your ten fingers and not one penny more. She should have seen that long ago and not slaved night and day, without a bit of sunshine, as she did. All her sweet youth blown through the window and for what? It didn't pay; she could by this time have something; but she was afraid to take chances. If she lost, who would help her? You didn't find money in the street. If you had a pocket full of money everybody was your friend, but if you were down and out nobody recognized you. Oh, well, she went on, God would help her and everything would come out all right. [Pp. 149–50]

Only the first chapters are devoted to Lizzie, but her emotional ambience controls Lorry and the book. When the narrator (and Lorry) is not in anguish over her irregular life, or dwelling upon her pathetically petty bourgeois values and "wisdom," he is clearly elegiac. Lorry and the narrator are not repulsed: they are in conflict over their heritage. This clash accounts for the passivity of Lorry—at times a kind of paralysis. The struggle central to and constant in *Bottom Dogs*, *Flushing*, and *Flesh* is between rejection and acceptance, repulsion and love, of the mother. In *Bottom Dogs* the various elements jostle one another: the narrator is so close to an experience that seemed unique, eccentric, and painful that the best he can achieve is an act of naming.

In *From Flushing to Calvary* Dahlberg closes upon his subject with more assurance. There is first of all the very much tighter structure. The action is complete, the scene more unified, the problem of mother-son identity more definitely in focus. Lorry's attraction and repulsion are dramatized in many small ways—by his fascination and despair, for example, with her petty Machiavellian shenanigans—and in the larger plan of the book. He insists she give up her barbering and come to live with him in New York; then he abandons her (to make a pilgrimage to the orphanage in a futile effort to resurrect spiritually a deceased surrogate father), only to return to New York in time for her death.

If the vernacular and the literary tend to jostle one another uneasily in *Bottom Dogs*, they are more clearly defined and separated in *Flushing*. The narrator commits no "errors" in diction and spelling, and he divides the literary and the vernacular worlds between Lorry and Lizzie (there is some mixing: Lizzie reads five pages a day of *Tom Jones*, chiefly to get "tony" words to use in answering matrimonial ads). Lorry is more clearly a word-man and aspiring writer in this book. "In the beginning was the word," he reflects at one point, reminiscing about his time in L.A.: "metempsychosis, metamorphosis, transmigration, protagoras, transcendentalism, swedenborgianism, swedenborgian fungi . . . de profundis, out of the depths, dorian dorian the portrait of dorian gray, théophile gautier, multifarious, asphodel, santa monica, capistrano, monterey, carmel-by-the-sea . . ." (pp. 72–73). *Flushing* is Dahlberg's portrait of the artist as a young man. Unlike Joyce's young man, who had been to school to the Jesuits and who could soar above the nets of religion, country, and family by committing himself wholly to his mythic father, the fabulous artificer, to art, Dahlberg's artist is an autodidact American, uncertain about even locating his country, family, religion. At the end, he can only commit himself to the road. Lorry's final snatch of a Macabbean stanza, "triumph, triumph crowns our glorious way," is therefore a bitterly ironic commentary on his sense of defeat rather than his exaltation. The road from Flushing—the dreary wasteland of Brooklyn and Long Island flats, his America—to Calvary produces a crucifixion but no apotheosis. The death of his mother follows the death of his hopes for a spiritual father, so the artist is completely orphaned.

Opposed to Lorry's life and its crises are the long sections devoted to the rhythm and pattern of Lizzie's days. They are the book's triumph; her voice and the vernacular tradition it embodies are the real strength of *Flushing*. In a language authentically her own—and recognizably the product of an American experience—she reveals herself in all her shabbiness and glory. Her language is full of Sunday supplement and backyard science and sophistication, the jargon and self-deception of the petite bourgeoise, the unexamined shards of a life lived close to the unliterary bone of American life. A sometime Machiavellian, a petty charlatan of homeopathic nostrums, her strength resides, finally, in her ability to accept the reality of the life she lives. She refuses to see it as irregular or odd; at whatever stage and with whatever oddball materials—the flotsam and jetsam of our urban civilization—she makes her communities. Lizzie's glory is that however much she seems to opt for money and advantage, she is always undone by her humanity: what she is really after, always, is respect, sympathy, love. Though she is the despair of Lorry Lewis, and behind him Dahlberg (we must assume), her death removes a vital force from his life and can only leave him desolate.

So the ambivalent relation to the mother is at the heart of this book. Besides the obvious Oedipal overtones, what I am trying to suggest is the cultural significance of the relationship: Dahlberg in a love-hate relationship with Lizzie Lewis's America. *Flushing* reveals a perfect tension between exorcism and celebration, an achieved dramatization of this problem. It is unjustly neglected as such, and as another document in the long tradition of American writers struggling to accommodate themselves to their complex fate.

Dahlberg has presumably repudiated these works of his suffering youth. A wholly different man appears in the later works, especially those concerned with "the dialogue with the body" in a voice that is prophetic when it is not crotchety. Yet the subject of his widely admired *Because I Was Flesh* is obsessively the same as in the two early works discussed and, although "different," the voice reveals elements present in one way or another in them. There are, however, two chief differences. First of all, Dahlberg can accommodate without a sense of strain his acute sense of the observed world and "the rude vernacular," with his vast learning and his penchant for high style, to the enrichment of both—an accommodation that sits easily with a generation of readers trained to Augie March and his literary descendants. It would seem that after thirty years, in this respect at least, Dahlberg and America may have come of age. That is, despite the rage in his prophetic works, Dahlberg's pain in accommodating himself to his two worlds has abated; he has come to terms—verbally, at least—with his mother and his life. The chief difference, and it probably makes all the difference, is Dahlberg's process of mythicizing and so both distancing himself from, and possessing, his past. That is, by placing his mother and his America within a context of timeless literature, religion, and mythology, he hopes to transform singularity to universality, shabbiness to glory, suffering and aspiration to aspects of man's eternal condition.

> Let the bard from Smyrna catalogue Harma, the ledges and caves of Ithaca, the milk-fed damsels of Achaia, pigeon-flocked Thisbe or the woods of Onchestus, I sing of Oak, Walnut, Chestnut, Maple and Elm Street. . . . Could the strumpets from the stews of Corinth, Ephesus or Tarsus fetch a groan or sigh more quickly than the dimpled thighs of lasses from St. Joseph or Topeka? [P. 2]

The earlier process of exorcism and celebration is being repeated— on a new level. Later in the book he recalls sitting in his mother's room in Kansas City, "filled with a fatherless emptiness" (p. 168), and asks further along, "Why was it impossible for me to let go of the misery of my boyhood?" (p. 220). He is able to "let it go" in this book, finally, because of this process of mythicizing. "Mother and father is one flesh," says Hamlet, and Dahlberg leans on Hamlet's logic (one of the book's chapter headings, ". . . and so, my mother," comes from Hamlet's speech) to resolve his quest for a past and an identity. His fatherless emptiness is filled in his beautiful and final acceptance of a mother who had been both mother and father.

> When the image of her comes up on a sudden—just as my demons do—and I see again her dyed henna hair, the eyes dwarfed by the electric lights in the Star Lady Barbershop, and the dear, broken

wing of her mouth, and when I regard her wild tatters, I know that not even Solomon in his lilied raiment was so glorious as my mother in her rags. Selah. [Pp. 233–34]

Dahlberg has accepted the gift and miracle of his life. *Selah*, and *shantih*.

Six

Elmer Rice, Liberation, and the

Great Ethnic Question

Writing back in 1932 about Elmer Rice, Meyer Levin—in what is still the best article on the once-celebrated playwright—quotes André Maurois, who said in *The Atlantic Monthly* that among dramatists who "ought to [be] read . . . [are] Eugene O'Neill and Elmer Rice."[1] Maurois was a figure of great contemporary authority; moreover, he was not the only one to link those two names. In the twenties and thirties Rice and O'Neill were often cited as proof of the coming of age of American drama since 1914—that convenient date for marking the end of American innocence, which happens also to be the year that O'Neill published his first volume of one-act plays and Rice, at the age of twenty-one, achieved instant success and a modicum of financial independence with his first play, *On Trial*. Both won international attention because of their stage innovations, chiefly, though certainly not exclusively, for their experiments with expressionist techniques. At the time of Levin's article, O'Neill's *Hairy Ape* and *Emperor Jones* were, of course, well known; Rice's *The Adding Machine* (1923) was still playing European art theaters; and Rice's Pulitzer Prize-winning *Street Scene* (1929) was widely regarded as "a superb documentation of American manners."[2]

From our contemporary perspective—O'Neill's reputation has

1. "Elmer Rice," *Theatre Arts* (January 1932), p. 54.
2. Ibid.

never been greater than it is now—that the two dramatists were once considered equals by critics of the first rank makes one wonder why there is such a paucity of material about Elmer Rice.[3] The question almost answers itself. If O'Neill had remained the playwright he was between the wars, he would very likely still rank above even his most gifted contemporaries (Sidney Howard, Robert Sherwood, Maxwell Anderson, Elmer Rice), but some of his early work looks quaint and hollow today, only of historical interest (*vide* Groucho Marx's deflation of *Strange Interlude* in one of his films). That is, if O'Neill had not gone on to write, out of his age and his anguish, *The Iceman Cometh* and that authentic American masterpiece, *A Long Day's Journey into Night*, he would be regarded as an interesting and worthy playwright, his work a measure of America's culture at a certain period, but not as one of the great dramatists on the world's stage. Elmer Rice, it must be said at once, never achieved that final breakthrough in his career. Mentioning O'Neill and Rice in the same breath both elevates and diminishes one's estimation of Elmer Rice and his achievement. It forces a generation to whom the name Rice is relatively unknown to pay attention; once we have read his plays, we find that we admire certain plays and certain intentions but are disappointed in others—some of his concerns and techniques seem dated and irrelevant. The causes of both reactions are worth exploring.

Today we ask who Elmer Rice is, or was, and why he should be remembered. At first glance, the rubric "Jewish-American dramatist" does not seem entirely germane. Other approaches—the scholars' straight theatrical history, or a formal analysis of his themes and concerns seen in their various contexts—certainly enable us to assess Rice relatively well.[4] But "the great ethnic question" (Henry James's phrase in *The American Scene*, which he coined

3. Jackson R. Bryer and Ruth M. Alvarez, "American Drama, 1918–1940: A Survey of Research and Criticism," *American Quarterly* 30, 3 (Bibliography Issue, 1978): 298–330. As the authors observe, "There is more material available about O'Neill than about all of the other playwrights of the 20s and 30s combined," and "there is a need for good critical essays on Rice" (pp. 321 and 324).

4. The most notable studies in a lean field are Ralph L. Collins, "The Playwright and the Press: Elmer Rice and His Critics," *Theatre Annual* (1948–49): 35–58, and the two books devoted to his work, Frank Durham, *Elmer Rice* (New York: Twayne, 1970), and Robert Hogan, *The Independence of Elmer Rice* (Carbondale: Southern Illinois University Press, 1965).

when he regarded New York's new population at the beginning of the century) may not be, if approached humbly, entirely irrelevant. Put crudely, out of elements in his ethnic and family drama confronted directly, O'Neill achieved a major, tragic vision. Elmer Rice, born Elmer Leopold Reizenstein, the grandson of German-Jewish immigrants, usually ignored his own "Jewishness" and produced out of his energy and talent a fine body of work, much of it innovative and brave, that lacks the mark of ultimate greatness.

Lest the equation I have presented be taken too simplistically, let me acknowledge at once all qualifications—not the least of which is the need to maintain a proper historical sense. That is to say, had Rice, in his time, attempted to habitually "confront" his ethnic situation directly (even if he wanted to), he might well have driven himself from the competitive stage.

This is not the occasion to enter into a long discussion of anti-Semitism and American culture in the formative years of Rice's growth and early success, but some historical data are necessary. In those years—from the turn of the century into the thirties—the general climate in the dominant culture, responding to its own insecurities in the face of dimly understood but vast and visible changes in the American culture and economy, especially the increasingly obvious presence of millions of immigrants and ethnics, closed ranks against the "outsider" and advocated something called 100% Americanism. As John Higham has shown, much of this generalized unease and hostility began to focus on the Jew. American anti-Semitism crystallized in the early twentieth century, peaked in the twenties (the era of a renascent KKK and the 1924 Johnson-Reed Act that restricted immigration upon racist and nationalist grounds), and was unusually intense in the late thirties—although by that time a broad movement for "ethnic democracy" had emerged to fight Father Coughlin, the Silver Shirts, and so on.[5]

During this time, the literary world was not free of the taint of anti-Semitism or unresolved ambivalences regarding the Jew, even in the work of major writers. Henry Adams's psychosis on the subject is well known, as is Dreiser's. Masterly works, the pride of

5. John Higham, *Send These to Me: Jews and Other Immigrants in Urban America* (New York: Atheneum, 1975), pp. 184–91.

American literature survey courses, like Wharton's *The House of Mirth*, Fitzgerald's *The Great Gatsby*, and Hemingway's *The Sun Also Rises*, are scarred by what the Jews in them are made to represent. On the stage, sentimentalized, stereotypic portrayals held sway—Lou Holtz, Dr. Kronkheit, Potash and Perlmutter may have been acceptable as funny vaudeville, but on the legitimate stage, the hit of the twenties had to be the kitsch of *Abie's Irish Rose*. In the face of all that, one is less surprised that a writer with Rice's skill at courtroom drama did not directly treat a subject like, say, the Leo Frank case (Frank was a northern Jew lynched in Atlanta in 1913, a year before Rice wrote *On Trial*). When Rice did explore the potential for mindless violence in the average man frustrated by forces beyond his comprehension, he did so in the more oblique and stylized expressionist manner of *The Adding Machine*, written ten years after the Frank lynching. Mr. Zero in his defense to the jury talks about dirty "sheenies" always getting two to the other fellow's one, but Rice's target in the play is even broader and more generalized than anti-Semitism, which is only one of Zero's deficiencies. A similar pattern recurs in Rice's other plays that touch upon Jews.

The date and title of Michael Gold's *Jews Without Money* (1930) might be taken as a turning point of sorts. The title directly refutes the general lie behind much of American anti-Semitism, and throughout the depression writers began to feel freer about using their ethnic origins as material—Odets's *Awake and Sing!* (1935) was among the first and best, as was Rice's even earlier and more commercial *Counsellor-at-Law* (1931). Broadway plays reached a small, relatively sophisticated audience—plays that were later made into mass-market films were often "de-ethnicized" in the process. Even as late as the forties, obviously Jewish material was deracinated, as the slightest reflection upon *Death of a Salesman* shows. We all *know* Miller's play is (or should be) about a Jewish salesman and his family, but in order to generalize its appeal, it seemed to be necessary to give the family no recognizable ethnic identity at all. This proved to be no impediment to its pop acceptance as an American classic. To be "American" was to remove the Jewishness—even as late as the postwar era. This obfuscation should not be surprising if we remember that according to Gallup, anti-Semitism was at its height in this country in the immediate postwar years and did not diminish significantly until after about 1947, when the full import of the Nuremberg Trials began to sink in.

But Jewish writers did begin to acknowledge their link to Jewish fate in the thirties under the increasing threat of German fascism. One thinks of the antifascist dramas of "nonidentifying" Jewish writers like Edward Dahlberg, Lillian Hellman, and especially Elmer Rice. I daresay no Jew, however attenuated his or her connection with Judaism, could feel that those German troops photographed by Movietone News marching down the Champs Élysées in the spring of 1940 were not coming directly after him/her. Something like that must have been the impulse behind Rice's *Flight to the West*, produced in December 1940. The protagonist, Charles Nathan, a serious young Jewish American, previously a pacifist (like Rice), tries to persuade his Gentile wife that personal participation in the fight against Nazi barbarity is necessary and proper. Interestingly enough, he is arguing not primarily as a Jew who feels he must combat anti-Semitism, but as a human being who feels he must defend all civilized values. That is, the Jew is not the primary target of the brutes, he is only one of their many targets, which include not only all humane and right-thinking people but also such institutions of civilization as the library of Louvain (Rice resurrects the anti-Boche sentiments of the First World War).

After the war, Rice wrote few plays of specific social consequence, although as a citizen he was embroiled in defense of civil liberties causes. In the period of his major impact as a *writer*, therefore, it can be said that given the real alternatives available to him and who he was, where Rice did confront his ethnic situation, directly and indirectly, he made the most of it. In fact, those plays upon which his reputation as a serious dramatist may rest—*The Adding Machine*, *Street Scene*, *Counsellor-at-Law*—significantly touch issues that would lie at the heart of such a confrontation.

II

First of all, something must be said about who Elmer Rice was and some of his achievements. Answering the charge that changing his name (which he did sometime around 1918) was an attempt to hide his background, Rice said in his characteristically level way, "I have never paraded my origin, but I have never tried to deny it."[6] He changed it, he said, simply because it was so hard to spell and pronounce, and besides it was "foreign sounding" and he had no emotional ties with it. In his personal contacts he claims never to have been influenced by race, nationality, or religion; and although in his long career as a civil libertarian he fought anti-Semitism (as well as Jewish groups who tried to prevent the showing of *Oliver Twist*), he says he personally never suffered from it.[7] He was the only child of parents who maintained a tenuous connection with Jewish religious observances (the last remnant was his mother's fasting on Yom Kippur) and who were all but assimilated. He was turned off by the hypocrisies of the religious life he saw around him on Manhattan's Upper West Side, where he grew up, and refused to be confirmed in the faith. He became a Shavian agnostic, by his own report, never turned back, and never regretted his position. He was in love with theater, ideas, the city.

This bare-bones version of his ethnic biography, if a little cool, would sound familiar to many another Jewish youth growing up in New York, despite the haze of nostalgia and fashion through which that experience is currently being filtered. The experience of being assimilated to a cosmopolitan image of enlightened values—rational, liberal, and humane—is also a common one for the Jewish intellectual. It was a source of Rice's liberated strength as well as, perhaps, a certain emotional thinness in some of his writing.

Rice was immersed in the theatrical and ideological concerns of his time. His first play was a tour de force of craft—a courtroom melodrama of no great significance except that it introduced the flashback technique expertly to the stage, created a sensation, and made the young recent law graduate enough money that he could abandon a career he disliked for the life of a professional writer. His practical sense almost never deserted him, except that he fre-

6. *Minority Report: An Autobiography* (New York: Simon & Schuster, 1963). I have used the English edition of this enlightening book (London: Heinemann, 1963), p. 164.

7. Ibid., pp. 164–65.

quently pushed against the safe and accepted modes of thought and substance, as well as of craft and conventional modes of theatrical organization and financing—frequently against formidable resistance.[8] His great successes of the twenties, *The Adding Machine* and *Street Scene*, were produced and won their way only after considerable skepticism about their commercial or intellectual viability. In the thirties Rice played a heroic role that deserves an essay by itself. He was a key figure in the start of the Federal Theatre project, a crucial advisor to Harry Hopkins,[9] and became the first director of its New York section. He resigned in protest over the government's censorship of *Ethiopia*, one of the first *Living Newspapers*. In the late thirties he was one of the founders of The Playwrights Company (with Robert Sherwood, Maxwell Anderson, Sidney Howard, and others), which was short-lived but significant in its effort to elevate the country's commercial theater and its best writers. Throughout that period (and for the rest of his life) he was a mainstay of the American Civil Liberties Union, an important and active member of the Authors League, and a hardworking advocate of many liberal causes. He cites with pride his inclusion in Elizabeth Dilling's *The Red Network* (1934) and in *Red Channels*—both books were efforts to identify (some would say "smear") certain people in the media as reds, red sympathizers, or otherwise subversive types—although he was then and thereafter anticommunist and a pacifist.

It was a productive period, in which Rice attempted to broaden his range. He began the decade with a play that fizzled, *The Left Bank* (1931), a comedy about expatriates based on his sojourn in Paris in the twenties. This was followed in the same year by *Counsellor-at-Law* which, after *Street Scene,* was his longest-running play. He closed the decade with a charming comedy, *Two on an Island* (1940)—a love affair with Manhattan—that was a moderate success. In between, he experimented with ideological dramas, such as *We the People* (1933) and *American Landscape* (1938)—efforts to discern a positive American ethos during the depression years—the antifascist (and in my view fatally melodramatic) *Judgment Day*

8. *Vide*, Collins, "The Playwright and the Press."

9. Elmer Rice, *The Living Theatre* (New York: Harper & Bros., 1959). See ch. 13, "The Federal Theatre Project," especially pp. 150–53, his letters to Hopkins.

(1934), based on the Reichstag Fire Trial, and *Between Two Worlds* (1934), an effort to mediate between the communist and capitalist world-views. The later companion piece, *Flight to the West*, as already mentioned here, deals with the urgency of the Nazi threat. He was often lambasted for his ideological explorations—John Mason Brown thought (quite stupidly) that *Judgment Day* was as laughable as *The Drunkard*[10]—and many bitter exchanges between Rice and his critics in the *New York Times* and elsewhere led to Rice's announcement in 1934 of his retirement from the theater. Of course it didn't stick (he returned four years later), though he made several trips abroad, writing books about them, and he wrote at least one successful novel (*Imperial City*, 1937) to prove to himself he didn't need the stage.

In 1945 he produced one of his slighter but most charming and successful plays, *Dream Girl*, as a comic vehicle for his second wife, Betty Field. His first wife, to whom he had been married many years, was named Hazel Levy. It was a light treatment of a serious theme common to all his best works—the need to abandon moonshine and illusion, to come to grips with reality in a truly liberating way. He kept working through the fifties and sixties, writing more plays and books. At the time of his death in 1967 there were two plays left unproduced.[11] Even this brief outline shows that his was an extraordinary and interesting career. Its relevance as cultural history cannot be doubted and awaits a full-scale treatment. What follows—a brief consideration of his three most significant plays—is a mere prolegomenon, perhaps, to such a study.

III

Rice once wrote, in an apologia of sorts, that

> the dominant concern . . . of all of us . . . should be with the attainment of freedom of the body and of the mind through liberation from

10. Collins, "The Playwright and the Press," p. 53.

11. Hogan offers a most interesting appraisal of these, as he does of most of Rice's voluminous output. He makes a good case for adding to my small list of plays representing major achievement. See also his "Elmer Rice: A Bibliography" (*Modern Drama*, February 1966) for a listing of Rice's work from 1913 to 1965.

political autocracy, economic slavery, religious superstition, heredi-
tary prejudice and herd psychology and the attainment of freedom of
the soul through liberation from fear, jealousy, hatred, possessive-
ness and self-delusion. . . . Everything that I have ever written
seriously has had in it no other idea than that.[12]

His own assessment of what is the most significant and consistent
theme in his work cannot be faulted. Each of the plays I will consider examines and criticizes in its own way restraints upon human
freedom and liberation.

In *The Adding Machine* the central character is Mr. Zero, whose
name is meant to express his emotional, psychic, and social nothingness.[13] The stylized dialogue, rich in cliché and stereotype,
between Mr. and Mrs. Zero—and their friends the Ones, Twos,
Threes, Fours, Fives, and Sixes—reveals sexually repressed,
bigoted, narrow lives. After twenty-five monotonous, robotizing
years adding numbers in the office of a department store, Mr. Zero
becomes a victim of technological advance and is fired. Shocked for
once into significant action, in his rage he kills his employer. He is
tried and convicted by a jury of his peers (the same Ones, Twos,
etc.) and executed. In the Elysian Fields after death, he is vouchsafed a brief experience of sexual and emotional liberation with
Daisy Devore, a fellow worker who has killed herself for love of
Zero. Finally, he is offered the chance by the heavenly powers to
return to earth as a more liberated person, but he rejects the opportunity and chooses to go back as the craven self he was before.

On its most profound level, in its portrayal of the timid little
man fearful of freedom, the raw material of lynch mobs and fascism, Rice's *Adding Machine* anticipates the classic analyses of
Wilhelm Reich in *The Mass Psychology of Fascism* and Erich Fromm's
Escape from Freedom. But he does not probe as consistently as they
do the social and psychological roots of this kind of behavior. At
best Rice suggests obliquely that there may be such roots, but for
the most part he is content to present as a given Zero's character
structure, which he then exploits theatrically and ideologically.

12. In a *New York Times* piece (25 December 1938), quoted in Hogan, "Elmer
Rice," p. 16.
13. The text cited is *Elmer Rice: Three Plays* (New York: Hill and Wang, 1965).

Why, when he has the opportunity to change at the end does Zero revert to slavish conformism once again? Well, says the heavenly functionary, "the mark of the slave was on [him] from the start." On the face of it, this judgment is too glib, too elitist, too despairing.

Such a judgment is strongly reinforced in the many long speeches in the play's last scene by this same heavenly emissary, who presumably provides out of his cosmic understanding the ultimate meaning of it all. He says,

> You're a failure, Zero, a failure. A waste product. A slave to a contraption of steel and iron. The animal's instincts, but not his strength and skill. The animal's appetites, but not his unashamed indulgence of them. True, you move and eat and digest and excrete and reproduce. But any microscopic organism can do as much. Well—time's up! Back you go—back to your sunless groove—the raw material of slums and wars—the ready prey of the first jingo or demagogue or political adventurer who takes the trouble to play upon your ignorance and credulity and provincialism. You poor, spineless, brainless boob—I'm sorry for you! [P. 61]

Desite the mild expression of sympathy at the end, Zero stands indicted for his unchanging and slavish nature. But that is not quite all there is to it—as might be the case in a rigorously expressionistic drama of the twenties. To the two-dimensional portrait of an early Archie Bunker character, Rice adds many humanizing touches; more to the point, the play is fun to read, play, and see.

In support, one is tempted to quote extensively whole monologues, dialogue, scenes. Mrs. Zero's opening monologue in bed (a repressed and nasty Molly Bloom) and Zero's peroration to the jury are masterful evocations of a way of life, self-indicting but involving us as well ("Suppose you was me, now. Maybe you'd 'a' done the same thing. That's the way you oughta look at it, see? Suppose you was me—" [p. 24]. The jurors, of course, rise as one and venomously declare him "Guilty!" There are touching moments—Zero, enjoying his wife's ham and eggs as his last meal, or Zero and Daisy in the Elysian Fields (and never out of character: Daisy says, "Look at the flowers! Ain't they just perfect! Why you'd think they was artificial, wouldn't you?"). Shrdlu, whom

Zero meets after death, is a marvelous character (he was played in the original production by Edward G. Robinson). He is a mild-mannered murderer, surprised that one Sunday, at dinner with the minister, he stuck the carving knife into his mother's throat instead of the weekly leg of lamb. In heaven he is dismayed that the only ministers admired seem to be Dean Swift and Abbé Rabelais, for their indecent tales, and that the people there think of nothing but enjoyment and wasting their time in such profitless occupations as painting, sculpting, composing songs, and writing poems.

Rice is writing here out of his cosmopolitan urbanity. He reflects an American twenties' sensibility that owes as much to Mencken's attacks on the American "booboisie" and provincial philistinism as to German expressionism. There is a tension between the two modes: Rice may appear too facile in trying to accommodate both, but it assures the play life beyond its ideology. By manipulating our empathy with Zero—by humanizing him, making us complicit in his fate—the play becomes something more than a thesis-ridden cautionary tale. His background made it inevitable that Rice would be one of the enlightened anti-Puritans of his day. Out of that reality, Rice domesticated expressionism to his American language and assumptions, giving us, thereby, a continually relevant appeal to self-examination. The play is satiric and caustic, but its despair is only superficial, belied by Rice's witty, bedrock commitment to living and human values.

Street Scene is a lovely play, despite its dated, sensationalistic, and stereotypic qualities.[14] For those unfamiliar with Samuel Goldwyn's faithful early thirties screen version or the operatic adaptation by Kurt Weill (lyrics by Langston Hughes), the play's chief elements can be briefly noted.

The entire action takes place during a summer evening and the following morning and afternoon on a one-set stage that represents the street fronting an ugly New York brownstone tenement whose stone steps, front door, first- and second-story apartment windows dominate the scene like the temple or royal entrance in Greek tragedy. The plot turns on a horrifying act that takes place in one of

14. I use the Samuel French edition of *Street Scene* (New York, 1929), although it is conveniently available in *Three Plays*.

the apartments. A stagehand, Frank Maurrant, shoots and kills his wife and her lover, a milk-money collector. Maurrant is pursued, caught, arrested, and led off to a certain execution. Much of the play's interest focuses on the interplay among the various tenants, who comprise practically a cross-section of New York's white ethnics.

Street Scene was first produced in January 1929, before the Crash and the Great Depression. At the time few professional theater people believed that a play dealing with such depressing fare and so mundane a milieu could succeed. In fact it did, phenomenally— and if we now decry what became the stereotypes and stock situations that were staples of drama and films for the next twenty years, we must acknowledge Rice's genius in originally creating them or at least realizing their dramatic potential. First of all, *Street Scene* was a superb piece of stagecraft. The set (designed by Jo Mielziner) was visually imposing; the use of only one set made for fluidity of pace; incorporating the city's sights (excavations, warehouses) and sounds (traffic, sirens, street games) was imaginative; and the variety of character types maneuvered gracefully through hundreds of difficult entrances and exits was simply breathtaking. It was Rice's first effort, almost against his will, as a director, and it was a triumph. More significant, the plunge into New York's ethnicity, for the purpose of a serious exploration of contemporary realities, and not just comic relief, gave the play much of the authenticity and power it can still convey.

Rice was still caustic about the Zeroes of ordinary life—Mr. Zero's worst characteristics appear in both Maurrant (but with differences) and, especially, the Jones family. The Joneses, despite their name, are bigoted Irish and so unrelievedly awful they are wonderful. Father drinks and misses work; mother is the archetypal malicious busybody and gossip, doting on her two despicable children, Vincent (a coarse bully who drives a cab) and May (a drunken slattern). They have a dog named "Queenie." As their name suggests, they transcend ethnic stereotyping; they have no redeeming social value; they endure.

A cheerful Italian musician named Fillipo Fiorentino and his fat German wife Margharita (he is enormously affectionate toward her, although she regards her childlessness as a constant reproach) live on one side of the entrance hallway, a Jewish family on the other. Abraham Kaplan is an old radical writer for the Yiddish press; his sensitive son Sam, who quotes Whitman, is in his last year of college and on his way to law school; his daughter Shirley is described in the stage directions as "an unattractive Jewess"—she is a schoolteacher, supporting Sam through college. The janitors are Scandinavian (in the opera they are black—that way Hughes could write a blues song for them). It is unclear whether the Maurrants are Irish-Catholic or Protestant, but the husband Frank is a "law and order" man, whose ideas are of the sort that used to be associated with the Hearst press. His wife Anna is sweet and touching, a gentle soul yearning for tenderness to grace her life. Their young son Willie is a kid growing up tough in the streets. Their daughter Rose (played in the original production by Erin O'Brien Moore, with what must have been unbearable beauty) is the play's strongest character. She speaks some of its best lines as she rejects crass suitors, feels for and advises Sam, comforts her mother (and ultimately her father), and assumes responsibility for Willie and a new life at the end.

Rice captures perfectly the New York period flavor in his scenes on the front "stoop" on a hot summer's night. The tenants come out to eat ice cream, cool off, and banter among themselves. Then suddenly serious issues are touched, raw nerves and the roots of character exposed. Discussing a recent eviction, in which the land-lord had been a Jew, Mr. Kaplan offers his doctrinaire socialist analysis of the event (which has to do with capital and not ethnic issues). Maurrant takes exception: "Well, we don't want no revolutions in this country, see?" to which there is a "general chorus of assent." The Joneses jump in to denounce free love, godlessness, the teaching of evolution. Shirley defends everyone's right to his own opinion. "Not if they're against law and order, they ain't," replies Maurrant. "We don't want no foreigners comin' in, tellin' us how to run things." At which Mrs. Fiorentino mildly demurs, "It's nothing wrong to be a foreigner. Many good people are for-eigners." And so it goes.

Momentarily thrown off by the offense given by the foreigner remark, and a mock-serious discussion between Olsen and Fioren-tino about who really discovered America, Maurrant and Jones get back on their track with a version of reality that all but the Kaplans can agree on: "Like I heard a feller sayin'," says Jones, "the Eye-talians built New York, the Irish run it an' the Jews own it." [Laughter] "Yeah," says Maurrant, "an' they're the ones that's doin' all the kickin'." Shirley responds with dignity, "It's no disgrace to be a Jew, Mr. Maurrant." To which he replies in Mr. Zero fashion—a mixture of right-wing platitudes and hysteria about freer sexuality—that seems to miss entirely the import of Shirley's remark:

> I'm not sayin' it is. All I'm sayin' is, what we need in this country is a little more respect for law an' order. Look at what's happenin' to people's homes, with all this divorce an' one thing an' another. Young girls goin' around smokin' cigarettes an' their skirts up around their necks. An' a lot o' long-haired guys talkin' about free love an' birth control an' breakin' up decent people's homes. I tell you it's time somethin' was done to put the fear o' God into people. [Pp. 55–56]

Rice is deftly pointing to the irrational connection between these barely repressed anxieties and anti-Semitism. In response to her husband, Mrs. Maurrant quietly observes, "Sometimes I think maybe they're only trying to get something out of life." This innocuous observation elicits an emotionally brutal reaction from him that underscores his inability to understand or fulfill her needs and that shows again his own intense inner pressures. These pressures finally explode when Kaplan utters another doctrinaire line about the abolition of the family once private property is abolished:

> MAURRANT [Belligerently]: Yeah? Is that so? No reason to exist, huh? Well, it's gonna exist, see. Children respectin' their parents an' doin' what they're told, get me. An' husbands an' wives, lovin' an' honorin' each other, like they said they would, when they was spliced—an' any dirty sheeny that says different is li'ble to get his head busted open, see? [P. 57]

Indeed we see. The scene stops just short of its threatened violence, but its potential hovers in the air over Maurrant. Years before Adorno's famous study of the authoritarian personality, Rice explored its roots in frustration at the sense of things getting out of hand, the scapegoating that substitutes for real control of one's life, the fear and insecurities that underlie rigidity.

Rice does not idealize his non-Jewish ethnics, to whom anti-

Semitism and its ugly epithets ("kike," "sheeny," "kike bastard") are pretty much taken for granted. They give ready assent to current notions of Jewish money-worship (along with their "bolshie" proclivities), but in the portrayal of Maurrant and beyond him, Rice sees their prejudice as only one of many undesirable results of a culture that supports rigid upbringing and demagogic indoctrination instead of reason, tolerance, and intelligence.

Significantly, the Jewish family stands out as a bastion of precisely those values that can humanize and transform the culture. The father seems doctrinaire in his unrelenting application of socialist analyses to every facet of the life around them—his own family is obviously so loving and supportive, could he really envision the demise of so bourgeois an institution "after the revolution?"—but he speaks out of Yiddish socialism's unwavering desire to see life constructed on more humane foundations than crass capitalism could provide to the spiritually and physically impoverished of America's ghettoes. Unlike the other tenement dwellers, Kaplan invariably speaks in the voice of reason and intelligence—to which his son Sam adds poetry and warmth, and a desire for transcendent love that is a bit moony but nevertheless touching. His sensitivity is in stark contrast to the emotional brutality of Olsen, Maurrant, and Jones. His Irish Rose responds to him and mothers him, but she does not marry him. Both she and Shirley urge upon him the need to continue his studies and rise from the life they all are forced to live. Rose will sacrifice for her brother Willie, as Shirley does for Sam. Although a spinster, Shirley is a prototypical ghetto or immigrant mother. She finds fulfillment and dignity in holding the family together (which includes a strong injunction against intermarrying); she is sane, stable, self-sacrificing. Her virtues and strengths stand in sharp contrast to the other women in the play, even Rose, who is wonderful but must contend with forces disintegrating her family that simply do not arise in the Jewish family before us.

Finally, Rice extends sympathy even to the murderer Maurrant. Despite his monstrousness in the scenes quoted, one can feel pity for his general air of bafflement as he tries to affirm what he regards as eternal verities. His values, unlike Zero's, as well as his murderousness stem from his character and do not represent an ideological ploy of the playwright's. And his character is not wholly his own to shape. If that were not true, his final poignant scene with Rose, which is a tear-jerker, couldn't work:

MAURRANT: I ain't been a very good father, have I?
ROSE: Don't worry about that, pop.
MAURRANT: It ain't that I ain't meant to be. It's just the way things happened to turn out, that's all. Keep your eye on Willie, Rose. Don't let Willie grow up to be a murderer like his pop.
ROSE: I'm going to do all I can for him, pop.
MAURRANT: You're a good girl, Rose. You was always a good girl.
ROSE [Breaking down]: O pop!
[She throws her arms about his neck and buries her head against him. Maurrant sobs hoarsely.]

Rose had earlier enjoined her father to be more warm and loving toward his wife ("There's a difference between loving and belonging"). In his final scene Maurrant admits he knew his wife had been a gentle and tender woman, but he had been drinking and "I must have been out of me head." Things just sort of happen—although not randomly. The implication is clear that background, training, environment, and social factors generally are more significant in shaping human conduct than morality or will power. This naturalist orientation, along with much else in the play, anticipates Odets, Kingsley, Shaw, and other dramatists of the thirties. The naturalist strain is emphasized further in the final scene between Rose and Sam following her father's removal.

Sam, in love with Rose, asks her to run off with him. She refuses, on the grounds that if she were to have a baby, they would end up trapped in their emotionally impoverished circumstances, like all the others around them. She agrees with his sister that he has a better future if he goes to law school (Shirley, interestingly enough, is also against marrying "out of one's kind"). The clincher, however, is that she and Willie will have a better chance if they leave the city—a motif that will become central in plays of the next decade. She aspires to have a house of her own in Queens or Staten Island. The slum, or rather the urban environment of the inner city itself, emerges as the enemy of the good life.

Somehow this is rather disappointing. I am reminded of Pare

Lorentz's thirties documentary, *The City*, in which at the end of the film the order and cleanliness of the planned Greenbelt community is meant to be the desired antidote to the noise, congestion, and dirt of the city. Unfortunately, what emerges concretely in the film's images is the contrast between the vitality of city life and the sterility of the suburbs. In *Street Scene* no such contradiction arises—the image of the better life lies offstage and in the future, as it were, while evidence of the vitality of the given is there before our eyes. The strength and beauty of Rose radiates even for contemporaries: what matters, she says to Sam early in the play, is "not what you do but what you are." *Street Scene* deals, finally, with these archetypes of human desire, rather than with stereotypes, and will endure.

The "great ethnic question" looms larger and more explicitly in *Counsellor-at-Law* than in any other play by Rice.[15] The central character, George Simon, who came to America in steerage as a young child, is a self-conscious Jew who has risen to great success as a smart New York lawyer. His partner is an Italian, for whom he acquires a judgeship from his boyhood friend Peter J. Malone. Malone is an important Tammany politician, and shares a common bond of values with Simon against, as he says, "those guys that came over on the Mayflower [who] don't like to see the boys from Second Avenue sittin' in the high places. We're just a lot of riff-raff to them." The ethnics have a common cause in this play, produced two years after *Street Scene*, in 1931, the worst year of the depression.

Rice subtly probes the contradictions apparent in the confrontation of ethnic outsider and dominant culture. Simon remembers and respects his past—he is generous to the poor, helps people of all kinds from his old East Side neighborhood, dotes on his mother (whose speech is sprinkled with Yiddish words). He is no angel, of course—he makes a killing on the market because of a leak from the Supreme Court, and blackmails his WASP three-named rival who has the evidence to disbar him for malpractice. This shrewd, energetic, highly capable man is utterly incapable, however, of seeing

15. In *Seven Plays by Elmer Rice* (New York: Viking, 1950), a useful collection that is unfortunately out of print. It includes *On Trial*, *The Adding Machine*, *Street Scene*, *Counsellor-at-Law*, *Judgment Day*, *Two on an Island*, and *Dream Girl*. *Flight to the West* is available only in an out-of-print edition (New York: Coward-McCann, 1941).

through and repudiating his shallow but indisputably upper-class WASP wife, Cora. She is snobbish and fatuously condescending (as are her snotty children from a previous marriage) to George, his work, his staff, and his mother. He disdains the enervated parasitism of one of his clients from her class (who will become her lover), and milks another (Schuyler Vandenbogen—the names and people of this group are caricatures) for some of his unearned millions in behalf of a show-girl client, but he requires the status of his marriage as a mark of his arrival and success.

This situation is not an unfamiliar one. Rice captures the historic moment and the myth well: a man from the lower classes, gifted with energy, know-how, and vitality, pits himself against a decadent dominant class but yearns for its marks of an assured civilization. On their part, the upper class—or, more accurately, the dominant Anglo parts of the culture—could see in the immigrants and their descendants the gravest threat to what they presumed was American civilization. It must be remembered that *Street Scene* and *Counsellor-at-Law* appeared within a very few years after passage of the racist (and to a considerable extent, anti-Semitically fueled) immigrant restriction act of 1924.

The cultural tensions and stakes were indeed high. What, after all, was America, and who would speak for it, control it? In the original production of *Counsellor-at-Law*, the part of George Simon was played to perfection by Paul Muni, who had a short time before transformed himself from the Yiddish actor Muni Weisenfreund and as Paul Muni went on from this play to fame and fortune in Hollywood. When the play made the same trip, it was similarly transformed and symbolically cleansed of its highly ethnic flavoring. In the film version George Simon was played by John Barrymore. Intermarriage between Jewish men and Christian women was an emotionally charged issue then and was not often represented on the large screen. When it was, it was treated in the quasi-parodic style of Groucho Marx and Margaret Dumont.

Rice did the best he could with the materials at hand. He gave the public what it seemed to want, or what he could induce them to want—the illusion of real life in his set, lots of characters and human interest, plots and suspense culminating in the success of

George Simon—which a contemporary will more often than not only groan at. To some extent, *Counsellor-at-Law* is a behemoth of a vehicle, an old-fashioned play that seems trapped in its sets and story. Even in that form, however, it should be seen as fixing an important moment in the evolving consciousness of Jew and ethnic in America. The heart of the play is Elmer Rice's characteristic plea for the liberation of human potentiality, and the freeing of self from dehumanizing illusions. Paradoxically, one is not always sure Rice is entirely free of the illusions of his own liberation—the hubris of rationalism, the trap of the contemporaneous.

Flight to the West showed that Rice could write a play in which a Jewish character close to his heart could prepare for heroic action, but not quite from the center of his Jewishness. Charles Nathan has to earn his moral authority by almost martyring himself—instinctively leaping to the defense of a reprehensible Nazi. In this play and others written before the war, there are twists and paradoxes that Rice only half-confronted and explored. A few years later, if a serious social dramatist were to write about the fate of the Jews, knowledge of the Holocaust would call for a fuller confrontation—the result might be silence, or a drama of towering rage and tragedy. In the years after the war, Rice obviously could not achieve such a dimension—his first postwar play was *Dream Girl*. And so, he is not the Jewish O'Neill, perhaps never could be, but he left an estimable legacy and, as Maurois observed many years ago, ought to be read. Even in oblique confrontations, Rice illuminates a part of America's cultural landscape we must increasingly come to know and appreciate.

III

The Southerner as
All-American Writer

Seven

Realism, Cultural Politics, and

Language as Mediation in Mark Twain

Our classical realists in the period 1865–1900 sought, in one way or another, to grasp the essence of their new concern and method. Howells defined it as "nothing more and nothing less than the truthful presentation of material." Twain claimed in the preface of his first book, "I am sure I have written honestly, whether wisely or not," while James enjoined the aspiring writer in 1884 not to "think too much about optimism and pessimism; try and catch the color of life itself."[1] "Truth," "honesty," faithfulness to "the color of life itself"—what serious writer, in any period and writing in any mode, is not committed to those things? The problem, of course, lies in what we mean by each term—where are "the material" and "the color of life," and by what standards (and by whom) are they to be validated? The resolution of those questions is a version of cultural politics.

For literary expression adequate to this challenging period of social expansion and differentiation, fresh assumptions and methods, frequently a new language or mode of expression embodying new ways of thinking, feeling, and seeing, would have to emerge and be legitimated. In the work of Mark Twain, primarily,

1. William Dean Howells, *Criticism and Fiction* (New York: Harper and Bros., 1891), p. 73; Henry James, "The Art of Fiction" (in *The Portable Henry James*, ed. Morton Dauwen Zabel [New York: Viking, 1951]), p. 417; "Preface" to *Innocents Abroad* (in *Mark Twain* [New York: Library of America, 1984]), p. 3.

and that of Dreiser and Crane later in the period, this development can be seen in two frequently interlocked ways.

First, there is the demonstration of the superiority of experience and direct observation of the natural world and of human behavior as guides to reality—behind that, the great authority of science and fact, the underpinning of visible technological progress—over that of inherited literary versions of those realities. The inherited versions, in their debased popular forms or in the excessively remote abstractions of the high culture, would be found unreliable in negotiating the complex and shifting currents of American life, irrelevant at best, absurd and dangerous at worst. Second, by their inappropriate language shall you know them for the unreliable sign-systems they are. The contention and competition between sign systems, vocabularies, dialects, and languages within a culture are, at bottom, a form of cultural politics—a significant feature of a diverse and pluralistic society. In such a society, many groups or subcultures (as they are sometimes revealingly called) struggle to have a say, literally, in order to define their experience from their own, not an imposed, perspective—and thus to play a role in defining the culture as a whole. Principally, language and literature will thus be seen as a constitutive element of reality rather than a mere reflection of it. Such a view calls into question the mimetic conception of literature, usually invoked as the chief rationale of a realist literature. It also questions the simplistic Marxist notion of a split between the material base of reality and a superstructure of institutions and thought that are reflections of that base. In such a view, which invariably assumes the base to be "the real foundation" (Marx's phrase in English translation), literature (and all products of consciousness) is merely epiphenomenal, ultimately only to be understood in terms of the base. Utilizing the Frankfurt School conception of mediation, I claim for literature a more substantive and significant role: as the indispensable bridge over the gap between base and superstructure (if indeed the gap exists).[2] Furthermore, mediation is useful in defining the role of

2. See Fredric Jameson's discussion of mediation as "the strategic and local invention of a code which can be used about two distinct phenomena," *The Political Unconscious: Narrative as a Socially Symbolic Act* (Ithaca, N.Y.: Cornell University Press, 1981), pp. 41–42. Althusser and Gramsci have from their differing perspec-

a writer between cultures, as it were, and will be developed in this paper with special reference to Mark Twain.

II

Twain is a central figure in the development of an appropriate response to key elements of late nineteenth-century American cultural diversity. At his best he calls into question dead language, stock literary conventions, mindless adherence to outmoded values; creating as an alternative a fresh language and vision that embodies fidelity to the facts of nature and American experience in its ordinary and unromanticized reality. Twain seems to be the very artist Whitman calls for in *Democratic Vistas*—that appeal for an American literary Declaration of Independence (in 1871), much like Emerson's earlier appeal for an intellectual Declaration in his "American Scholar" address (1836). In the paragraph following upon his call for an American poetry "that is bold, modern, and all surrounding and kosmical, as she is herself," Whitman speculates about the places of origin and mode of expression of the poets-to-come, who occupy for him such a supreme place in his dream of a democratic culture ("they only put a nation in form," he exclaims):

> Today, doubtless, the infant genius of American poetic expression
> . . . lies sleeping far away, happily unrecognized and uninjur'd by
> the coteries, the art-writers, the talkers and critics of the saloons [*sic*],
> or the lecturers in the colleges—lies sleeping, aside, unrecking itself,
> in some western idiom, or native Michigan or Tennessee repartee, or
> stump speech—or in Kentucky or Georgia, or the Carolinas—or in
> some slang or local song or allusion of the Manhattan, Boston, Phila-
> delphia, or Baltimore mechanic—or up in the Maine woods—or off
> in the hut of the California miner, or crossing the Rocky Mountains,
> or along the Pacific railroad—or on the breast of the young farmers of
> the northwest, or Canada, or boatmen of the lakes. Rude and coarse
> nursing beds, these; but only from such beginnings and stocks, indig-

---

tives within Marxism all but demolished the old base-superstructure dichotomy. And Lacan has shown that language acquisition is primary.

enous here, may haply arrive, be grafted, and sprout in time, flowers of genuine American aroma, and fruits truly and fully our own.[3]

No matter that Whitman and Twain had "a mutual disregard" for each other, as Justin Kaplan puts it in his splendid biography. Twain was familiar with the Western idiom, the stump speeches and repartee of the South, and the hut of the California miner. From his unprecedented knowledge, social and linguistic, of much of the whole face of America, and his commitment, like Whitman's, to "American speech as the vehicle for literature,"[4] Twain would produce in the next decade *Huckleberry Finn*, the first great masterpiece of the American vernacular. That book, Hemingway later said, was the beginning of American literature—thus fulfilling, one might say, Whitman's call for a literary declaration of independence.

From one perspective, Twain's was a long career of opposition to, as he saw it, reality-falsifying or irrelevant literary and linguistic models. He conducted an almost life-long running battle with certain of these models: he pilloried (from his early *Roughing It* to his late "Fenimore Cooper's Literary Offenses") as insults to intelligence James Fenimore Cooper's vision of nature and civilization, noble savages, literary elegance; he claimed only half-facetiously that Sir Walter Scott's romances and version of feudal chivalry were a cause of the Civil War; he heaped scorn on Sunday-school books (as in "Story of a Bad Little Boy") as containing nothing connected with recognizable truth. Sentimental effusions, romances, and a mindless rhetoric of optimism, piety, and uplift, all of these debased popular taste, clouded perception, and rendered one incapable of dealing honestly with ordinary reality. The prevailing popular philosophy of his time, subsequently labeled "the genteel tradition" by Santayana (in 1911), offered a watered-down romanticism and transcendentalism, and a religiosity of "refinement" and "sublimity." This world-view—ideal, unsullied by crass realities—about, for example, sex, or the way money was

3. Walt Whitman, *Leaves of Grass and Selected Prose*, ed. John A. Kouwenhoven (New York: Modern Library, 1950), p. 504.

4. Justin Kaplan, *Walt Whitman: A Life* (New York: Simon & Schuster, 1980), p. 27.

made and lost, or elementary physical facts of life—was a constant source of send-up for native American humorists, out of whose tradition (essentially a counter-culture) Twain came. For comic effect they contrast the ideal, as seen from the genteel perspective, with everyday reality and fact.

Any literary models—but especially bad ones—as substitutes for observed and experienced reality can have more serious consequences, however, for both a serious literature and for life. Where Tom Sawyer sees "A-rabs," Huck sees a Sunday school picnic, and gets bored with the world of imagined reality. But when Tom, from his same incorrigible desire to impose bookish romance upon reality, reduces Jim to a stock figure in melodrama, Jim's moral stature and the book collapse. In Stephen Crane's "Blue Hotel," the Swede helps create the conditions of his own murder by inappropriately and insanely conceiving of an 1890s Nebraska town in terms drawn from reading too many dime novel versions of the American wild West. Dreiser's *Sister Carrie*, the book that writes finis to the nineteenth century and begins the twentieth, inhabits the world of quasi-genteel magazine rhetoric and assumptions in the chapter titles of the edition that has held sway for most of this century, which is ironically at odds with and belied by the best sections of the narrative—those that derive from the new world of documentary realism and investigative journalism. The new Pennsylvania edition, based more closely on Dreiser's original text, mercifully drops the chapter headings ("The Machine and the Maiden: A Knight of Today," "The Lure of the Material: Beauty Speaks for Itself").

In the late eighties, Howells theorized on this subject for his generation of realists. They must not "take the life-likeness out of [their characters] and put the book-likeness into them," he says in the essay cited earlier. If you want to render a grasshopper, reject the idealized one handed down in artistic and literary models, go directly to the real one in the grass, "the simple, honest, and natural" grasshopper. It would seem a simple and obvious truth to him and his followers. The basic problem, or task, was to adjust one's vision to see what in fact was there, in the world of observable reality, not what one would like to see or has been taught to see. To do otherwise is to court literary as well as literal disaster. In "Old

Times on the Mississippi," Twain's riverboat pilot (an archetype of freedom and majesty for Twain: "the only unfettered and entirely independent human being that lived in the earth," "a king without keeper") must rely on sharp observation, prodigious memory of fact, experience and not moonshine or illusion, if he is to keep the bottom of his floating world from being ripped out. In the world of practical necessities, an empirical, pragmatic approach to observable reality is essential. More on this paradigmatic work later. The other crucial element—inseparable from vision—of adaptation to the new realities of the period is the language one would employ to embody or express the vision. The search for an appropriate and apposite language will accompany the effort to achieve the best vantage point from which to see and validate what is.

II

To adapt Howells's observation about "book-likeness" and "life-likeness" explicitly to the realm of language: it would be "life-like" if it were true to speech and the vernacular (one side of Twain's concerns), but also life-serving, or life-preserving, if it adapted itself to functional or pragmatic needs rather than inherited aesthetic conventions (another side of his concerns, about which unlike later naturalists, he felt curiously ambivalent).

Twain dealt with the question of language on many levels. He often satirized the debased language of popular taste—as in "Story of a Bad Little Boy," or in the memorably awful "Ode to Stephen Dowling Bots, Dec'd"—and the language of the official, as it were, high culture of his day. The latter also occurs in much of his work, but the cultural stakes involved are nowhere more directly confronted, though covertly expressed, than in his "Whittier Birthday Speech" of 1877. The full story of this rich psychodrama of an occasion, in which Twain told his story at the very heart of Brahmin culture, in the presence of the most venerated sages of his day—Emerson, Lowell, Holmes, Longfellow, the lot—is told by Henry Nash Smith (in an article called "Poor Clemens's Hideous Mistake," later incorporated as chapter 5 of Smith's *Mark Twain: Development of a Writer*). I will simply review its most salient features, seeing them from my perspective.

"Poor Clemens's hideous mistake" (the phrase was his friend Howells's) was to miscalculate all the implications of his amusing and fanciful story—not see that it might be considered a form of ridicule of the work and personages of the venerated sages of American culture who sat in places of honor at the dinner honoring Whittier. As Twain told it, he wandered into the hut of a California miner (he seems to have had *Democratic Vistas* somewhere in mind!) during a tour he made some years earlier when he was first beginning to enjoy some small notice in the western states. He wanted to test his new literary *nom de plume*, his new persona and role as a man of letters. Much to his surprise, the miner, "a jaded melancholoy man of fifty," informs him that he was the fourth "littery" man in twenty-four hours to appear in the hut. After some hot whiskeys, the miner explains that three scoundrels named Emerson, Holmes, and Longfellow had recently departed (with his boots, too) after intruding upon him for an evening of drinking, gambling, and snatches of poetry that he interpreted as irrelevancies or insults. No matter that the narrator explains that "these were not the gracious singers to whom we and the world pay loving reverence and homage; those were impostors," the miner was "agoing to move . . . [because] I ain't suited to a littery atmosphere." Leaving aside the wonderful pun on the word "littery" and much else in this rich tale and its occasion, let me just underscore two problems Twain touches upon.

One is the inappropriateness of the language of the high culture to the ordinary facts of life. The imposters do use actual lines from the real poets' work (albeit occasionally misattributed—in itself a commentary on their interchangeability). Mr. Holmes's exhortation, after sizing up the cabin, to "build thee more stately mansions, / O my soul," elicits from the miner the cry that "I can't afford it, Mr. Holmes, and moreover I don't want to." When Mr. Emerson says, after watching the miner preparing bacon and beans, "Give me agates for my meat; / Give me cantarids to eat; / From air and ocean bring me foods, / From all zones and altitudes," the miner gets indignant and says, "Mr. Emerson, if you'll excuse me, this ain't no hotel." From one point of view those gracious singers whom Americans love and revere—those eminences all sitting there as Twain told his story—didn't know beans. Their diction and frame of reference was too transcendental, abstract—

out of touch with the realities of the miner and his world. There is thus an aggressive thrust to Twain's raillery. He is using the energy and concreteness of the vernacular to undercut the lofty pretentiousness of the all but official culture. It was a strategy Twain used often, of course, and brought to a high art.

And yet the miner is, after all, a kind of simpleton and fool to be taken in so easily by obvious impostors and pretenders. There is an implicit commentary on the deficiencies of *his* ideas, world-view, culture. Thus, and this is the second problem pointed up in the story, the deflating energy of the vernacular is balanced by its weakness in the realm of ideas. The vulnerability of Huck Finn, his finest vernacular hero, to impostors and frauds (in people, ideas, and value structures) is here prefigured.

Then there is the uneasy silence at the miner's final comments, put in the form of questions directed at the narrator: "Ah! Impostors, were they? Are you?" Twain's inability to answer—he simply concludes the story quickly at that point with an apology for perhaps exaggerating a bit here and there—is suggestive. The ambiguity of his own literary standing, his credentials as it were, has two faces—to the miner this "Mark Twain" may prove as inauthentic as the other literary personages to whom "poor Clemens" is in effect serving notice about potential irrelevance. But Twain *does* know and say *beans*, so there is covert aggression and assertion in the story, directed primarily at the very high culture waiting to embrace him—as it previously had Howells—and whose acceptance he yearned for as well. And so the exaggerated guilt he was to feel about the event afterward—as well as the secret satisfaction he was to express years later!

More generally put, and referring to my earlier conception of one kind of mediation, Twain's task was to mediate between the worlds of the vernacular and the official or high culture, sometimes uneasily, sometimes triumphantly. His success or failure can be measured in the area of language. At his best (as in *Huckleberry Finn*) he creates a new language that bridges the gap between the cultures. From this perspective, *Huckleberry Finn* can be seen as essentially a mediation between two worlds of language (and values embodied by them). It pretends to be the faithful rendering of the speech of the Missouri Valley in the 1840s, but of course it is not. It takes a good deal from that speech, the essentials perhaps, but eschews the effort to render dialect *exactly* on the written page. He creates the illusion of a lifelike rendering of such a language, rather than attempting a literal transcription which, as we all know, would be unreadable and hopeless from a literary standpoint.

The trick is to achieve an air of authenticity based on knowledge and respect for the inner values conveyed by the dialect, but to make it accessible to the general reader. If successful, as Twain was in *Huckleberry Finn*, the result will be a new linguistic instrument and the validation of new strata of culture. Twain knew, basically, what was at stake and he was intermittently successful in achieving these things in his practice. He did not have available to him, or develop, however, the philosophical and intellectual ground for its complete articulation.

As a mediator between the worlds of West and East, or between that of the ordinary people, expressing itself in ordinary speech (the vernacular), and that of the high culture (to whose definition of culture the ordinary people often deferred, having nothing in which they were confident enough to put in its place), Twain often had to seduce his audience—or audience*s*—into changing their expectations of what a true reading of American reality was about. What Twain had was the flexibility and humility to learn from, change, and *name* these new realities. If he couldn't sell it to his audiences, he would be dead as a writer. On a grander scale, if a nation's culture displayed consistently a wide gap between its consciousness of itself and its natural life, its literature would be disembodied, empty, all but dead.

Let me pin this idea down more concretely. On the simplest level, Twain shows in a story like "A Genuine Mexican Plug" (from *Roughing It*, 1871) how the pride and ignorance that prevents a cultivated Easterner from learning the meaning of words in a new environment *can* kill him. The narrator says, "I did not know what a Genuine Plug was, but there was something about this man's way of saying it that made me swear inwardly that I would own a Genuine Mexican Plug or die," and of course he buys the plug and almost does die trying to ride the unmanageable beast. The point is you had better know the code, read the signs, and know the language if you would survive in a new place. Post–Civil War

America was, of course, full of new places—geographically, politically, economically, socially. The situation is presented in a much more richly suggestive fashion—and I turn again to it—in "Old Times on the Mississippi," that marvelous series of the mid-1870s that opened up to Twain's imagination the world of Tom Sawyer and Huck Finn, perhaps the deepest reaches of his emotion and craft.

To the steamboat pilot on the Mississippi, life and fortune depended literally and without comic exaggeration upon his ability to read the river correctly and precisely. In this enterprise, fact, knowledge, experience, and sharp observation of objective conditions were, as I noted earlier, crucial. Reliance on romantic illusions was potentially deadly. The pilot was expected to master and remember twelve hundred miles of complicated and shifting elements—and then, as the young cub apprentice says, "he must learn it all over again in a different way every twenty-four hours." Twain has here constructed a wonderful metaphor for the panoramic montage, the open, changing, shifting character of American life itself—and of the writer as pilot, whose skill and sharp knowledge would steer us safely through its shifting currents. Intriguingly, he sees the River and America as texts, to be read and interpreted—the hermeneutic implications are everywhere in "Old Times."

"The face of the water became in time a wonderful book. . . . There never was so wonderful a book written by man. . . . When I had mastered the language of this water . . . I had made a valuable acquisition." This wonderful book of the river (read America, Life, Reality) "was a dead language to the uneducated passenger, . . . but told its mind to me without reserve, delivering its most cherished secrets as clearly as if it uttered them with a voice." Elsewhere he compares learning the river to being able to read the Old and New Testaments backward and forward.

This language of Twain's is extraordinary here, tempting one to a reading of him as putative Kabbalist or mystic, and awaits the interpretation of a Viola Sachs.[5] For our purposes, the significance

5. See the interesting interpretation by Viola Sachs, "The Gnosis of Hawthorne and Melville: An Interpretation of *The Scarlet Letter* and *Moby Dick*," *American Quarterly* 32, 2 (Summer 1980): 123–43.

may be less arcane, more down-to-earth. First of all, we mustn't discount Twain's desire to elevate the job of piloting and with it his own background and credentials. It was his Harvard and Yale, much as the whaling ship was Melville's. The majestic, scientific, professional qualities are emphasized—no mention that steamboats could be filthy gambling dens (and worse)—as he suggests in a lurid moment in *Huck Finn* when Pap is found dead on the wreck of the Sir Walter Scott [*sic*]. Written for the pages of *The Atlantic*, "Old Times" was part of Twain's bid for a higher form of acceptance in the official culture than as Western roughneck, exotic, or "phunny phellow." To a large degree he succeeded, thereby validating a new sensibility, a new way for the writer to "be-in-the-world." Second, the key to reading the language of the river, the knowledge that penetrates its secrets, is scientific, as science was then understood—positivist, based on fact—and not esoteric (although there is room for intuition). Such a science was to take America far in the nineteenth century, certainly in material terms, helping it to achieve its leading role in the world's economy by 1900, and had achieved an authority over religious views it was never really to lose.

As our literary pilot, Twain achieves at his best a mode of interpreting that enables one to understand and survive fairly well the River/America. Respect for empirical reality, for the complexity, shifts, and changes that are part of it; flexibility and the humility to learn afresh, the mind free of damaging and dogmatic presuppositions.

What he does not fully grasp or articulate is that all language systems, as the new linguistics has taught us, are arbitrary, depending for their efficacy upon shared assumptions, conventions, understanding about purposes and functions. Language is thus not a reflection of reality but an expressive and constitutive part of it. Given such a conception, Twain would not be beset by the continuing perplexity he speaks of in "Old Times." He wonders at one point if he has lost more or gained more by his knowledge of the river. His analytic and scientific knowledge has taken all the "grace, beauty and poetry" from the river. In evidence, he submits a description of a sunset on the river whose beauty is lost to him now that he must describe it in the most functional terms appropriate to his task of getting the boat up the river. What is apparent, however, is that his description of "beauty" is undercut because it depends on the very rhetoric of sentimental calendar and chromoart that he is otherwise at pains to deflate. His perplexity would vanish if he had available to him a new set of conventions and assumptions *about* the nature of beauty. He needs to be able to incorporate a thinking, knowing observer, rather than the "bewitched" observer whose mind must almost consciously be numbed, knowledge eradicated, falling back rapturously upon a received convention of the beautiful.[6] This pilot has taken us a long way, pointing up weaknesses and dangers in ways of thinking, perceiving, and expression untested by contact with a fuller American reality, but his faith in his own vision is not always secure and unambivalent.

III

Between Twain and later writers like Crane and Dreiser there is a link, but also the difference that came with their being a younger and newer generation. Both born in 1871 (the year of *Democratic Vistas*), they were recipients by inheritance, as it were, of the full achievement of the realist vision, as well as the more rigorously based scientific faith of the naturalism that grew from it. But a crucial distinction must be made. Neither Dreiser nor Crane were mere offspring of Zola; they were shaped by their lived American reality.

Zola's attempt at a scientific appraisal of human behavior was based, as we know, upon the work of Claude Bernard—a scientific model that was essentially *static*, allowing for no changes in time. Probably the crucial influence upon Crane and Dreiser derived from their experience as journalists, and owed a lot albeit indirectly to the seminal example of Jacob Riis's *How The Other Half Lives* (1890). The era they grew up in valued a form of investigative journalism (as we would call it today) and developed a style con-

6. See Leo Marx's excellent essay on the significance of Twain's use of the vernacular in *Huck Finn* to resolve the dilemmas and perplexity felt in the "Old Times on the Mississippi" passage. Leo Marx, "The Pilot and the Passenger: Landscape Conventions and the Style of *Huckleberry Finn*," *American Literature* 28 (May 1956): 129–46.

sistent with that, which I will call, on the example of Riis's work, a version of documentary realism. The emphasis was upon dates, facts, objective evidence, the concrete. The crucial difference from Zola's model was that 1) journalists were aware that the facts might change or shift, and one would have to go out and do the story again—or like Twain's pilot, "learn it" all over again, and 2) there was often a purposeful and reformist intention behind the documentation of reality—it was not morally neutral, in a way positivist science might pretend to be. Dreiser's account of the death of Hurstwood, especially the chapter called "Curious Shifts of the Poor," his reworking of a journalistic piece on the Bowery, shows the method put to exemplary use in fiction. The writing is simple, direct, achieving great authority by its careful accretion of linked facts, becoming a powerful statement about the pathos of human existence. Dreiser, of course, would become an important pilot for later generations of writer-interpreters of American reality, as was Stephen Crane, whose "Bowery Sketches" parallel Dreiser's.

Crane's link to Twain was suggested earlier in his similar effort to show the danger of perceptions distorted by bad literary models. His best known story, "The Open Boat," shows further affinities with Twain's concerns—chiefly that surviving shifting, changing, potentially destructive conditions requires a view that is clear-eyed, unsentimental, and rooted in the situation you are *in*, not some other imagined or conventionally sanctioned perspective. Further along than Twain, however, in the intellectual and emotional currents of his era, he could accept this as the sufficient precondition of grace and beauty—or at least not worry about any other possible standard of beauty (insofar as that even comes into question).

In the famous opening lines of "The Open Boat" there is an unequivocal acceptance of the realist perspective. "None of them knew the color of the sky. Their eyes glanced level, and were fastened upon the waves that swept toward them." No time for innocent swoons of rapture at conventional images of nature's grandeur—a level view of the waves is primary, essential to survival. The larger implications of Crane's metaphor of the boat adrift on an open and amoral sea, based on his own real-life experience in a shipwreck, is of course existential and contemporary: we may all be shipwrecks afloat in an indifferent and amoral universe. That is the truth of things, his narrative tells us, from within the experience. "As each salty wall of water approached, it shut all else from the view of the men in the boat . . . *viewed from a balcony* [my italics] the whole thing would doubtless have been weirdly picturesque. But the men in the boat had no time to see it, and if they had the leisure, there were other things to occupy their mind." The picturesque did not exist for them—nor should it: Crane can dismiss it with a phrase, whereas Twain worried it for paragraphs and pages. As for sunrise, that bewitching staple occasion for an outmoded language and imagery of "beauty" (as in Twain), Crane's castaways "were aware only of [its] effect upon the color of the waves that rolled toward them." Again the question of perspective, purpose, and function as determinants of an appropriate perception and response—to the natural world, and beyond that to individual and social experience. The view from the crest of a wave "was *probably* splendid . . . *probably* glorious" [my italics], but to whom, and in what condition of removal from the real facts of life-and-death existence? For those who went through it, Hemingway (the heir of Twain and Crane) was to say in one of his stories about the First World War, certain abstractions, like "glory," would be forever impossible, and only the names of concrete places, battles, had any validity.

For Crane there is an implicit aesthetic in all this, which, unlike Twain, he does not question. In addition to its terrible threat, "there was a terrible grace in the move of the waves," says the narrator of "The Open Boat," and no one can read this story without assenting to *its* terrible grace (I am deliberately calling attention to the echo of Hemingway's emphasis on grace and style in facing hard realities). A thorough formal analysis could show that the *work*, in its strength of language and achieved form, is not merely a reflection of reality—though it comes out of Crane's profound experience of it—but is a version that we may assent to as apt for most of the reasons I have touched upon, and is like language itself a constitutive element of reality.

I hope my use of the principle of mediation has demonstrated its conceptual utility as a way to avoid the dilemmas of a mimetic conception of literature and of a simplistic base/superstructure notion of reality. In my brief examples from Twain's work (and others) I have shown that language/literature as aspects of consciousness do not reflect reality but are embodiments of realities and values systems, and *express* history and culture. By their skill, by striking resonant chords in their readers' sensibilities, writers legitimate versions of reality. Furthermore, when there are conflicting or competing claims or systems of value, culture, and language, there are writers who may mediate between them. If successful in this other aspect of mediation, the writer changes irrevocably the whole constellation we call culture.

That is what Crane and Twain achieved—calling into question one system of encoding and reading reality (the meaning of the sun upon the water, or of waves and ripples on its surface), creating another. Reading them in the context of their time they can convince us that a documentary, factual, direct apprehension of experience unfiltered through romantic literary models or idealist and pious illusions were needed to understand American reality and with a little luck, to bring one through dangerous waters. Of course, in our time, mere empiricism is suspect, inadequate in a world of quantum and contingency; and the faith in the possibility of a direct apprehension of experience seems naive. We are more aware than either of them (although Twain had premonitions) of the dark underside of science, technology, and the efficacy of mind—and of critical theory's critique of positivism and empiricism generally. Still, within time-conditioned limits, they remain unusually reliable pilots for at least beginning the negotiation of America's always moving waters.

The idea of competing versions of reality embodied in language and literature brings me back to some of the earlier concerns expressed in this book. How to understand the work of certain nineteenth-century writers usually labeled "regionalist" (Cable and Chopin) and "ethnic" (Cahan and Chesnutt)? What should emerge from this essay is the notion that an important way to view American social and cultural reality, or indeed that of any pluralistic culture, is as a mosaic (or a battleground) of competing cultural constituencies. Each will attempt, as I have said, to say things from the perspective of his/her own assumptions and linguistic integrity. A form of cultural politics is always involved in the process. When Howells enthusiastically welcomed Cahan's *Yekl*, it was largely on the basis of the language of the narrator—the standard American language, Howells said, which Cahan had become "naturalized to." Howells was reassured that Cahan (and the sensibility he represented) was no threat to the cultural center Howells by then represented—ignoring in his important review of the book the quite different story told by Cahan's characters in their own languages. In my view, it is in the sensitive investigation of just these linguistic nuances, and in the cultural politics of the interchanges among competing value systems, that the most reliable interpretation and understanding of American life, literature, and culture is to be achieved. If the knowledge required to achieve these readings seems daunting, we must reflect that "knowing" the Mississippi seemed even more impossible, yet the cub did become the pilot, and young Sam Clemens became Mark Twain.

Eight

Thomas Wolfe and the Cult of Experience

Thomas Wolfe has often been linked with Walt Whitman, that archetypal bard of the American experience, and in the late 1950s, there was a tendency to link the name of Jack Kerouac with that of Wolfe. There are obvious and inevitable reasons for thinking of Whitman as an ancestor and comrade of Wolfe's, and superficial reasons for linking his name with Kerouac's, and, by extension, with the world of "the Beats." Now he is often seen only as an ancestor—sometimes embarrassing—of other Southern writers. I should like to see him restored as an honorable ancestor—and not just for Southerners. Both the backward and the forward look from Wolfe are on the surface plausible strategies and may be profitable ways in which he may be seen clearly. That is, I think we will see certain fundamental differences in these writers which will enable us better to see Wolfe's unique features. In the process, some light may be shed on the perennial problem of the writer's attitude toward experience and his means of rendering it.

As early as 1930, one year after the appearance of Wolfe's first novel, *Look Homeward, Angel*, Sinclair Lewis, in his unprecedented and generous praise of young American writers in his famous Nobel Prize acceptance speech, struck off the key phrase in regard to Wolfe, calling him "a Gargantuan creature with great gusto of life." The image thereafter of a man consuming whole gobs of life, cramming and inflating himself with experience, out of sheer exuberance and love for it, stayed with Wolfe. Certainly, it contained a goodly measure of truth, and as surely made his identification with Whitman inevitable—that is, with the Whitman who claimed he was "large" and "contained multitudes."

Whitman had said in his Preface to *Leaves of Grass* (1855) that "the United States themselves are essentially the greatest poem," and that "it awaits the gigantic and generous treatment worthy of it." Whitman called for a poet capable of absorbing his country, who would then be generously and affectionately absorbed by his country.

Well, first of all, Wolfe seemed, even on the physical level, to be endowed with just the capacity to provide the gigantic and generous treatment called for by Whitman: he was six-feet-six, and an omnivorous devourer of books, food, and experience. Wolfe himself uses the image of the "absorber" when he speaks approvingly of his alter ego George Webber's "being like a sponge," who, furthermore, "made use of everything he absorbed." The reception afforded Wolfe's first work probably helped to consecrate him in precisely the role Whitman had called for as bard and chronicler of the American experience. That is to say, it seems clear that the reception of *Look Homeward, Angel* helped Wolfe to execute an "about-face" from a Mencken-Lewis-oriented skeptical vein in his earliest literary efforts, toward his assuming the stance of a serious, dedicated, conscious artist of America who would, as Richard S. Kennedy observes, use his "grasp (of) the variety of American life . . . to celebrate his nation."[1]

That is, in reading of his life, one has the sense that Wolfe was somewhat amazed by the reception of his book as a great American chronicle. After all, that first book was, as we all know, intensely autobiographical, and in some ways limited geographically; it is certainly unsurprising in its theme of the young man seeking to break free from the bounds of family and region toward a larger area in which to fulfill his expanding sense of self and life; and it was written, in some considerable part at least, out of the impulse to pay off old scores and as an art of self-healing (see Kennedy's and Elizabeth Nowell's biographical accounts of the book's genesis and execution).[2] How then, and why then, should such a book inspire

1. Richard S. Kennedy, *The Window of Memory: The Literary Career of Thomas Wolfe* (Chapel Hill: University of North Carolina Press, 1962), p. 192.

2. Elizabeth Nowell, *Thomas Wolfe: A Biography* (New York: Doubleday and Co., 1960).

critics to acclaim and herald Wolfe as the man who might write "the Great American Novel"? The answer, of course, is supplied by Sinclair Lewis, again, who said in a newspaper interview that Wolfe's "first book is so deep and spacious that it deals with the whole of American life."[3] The key here lies in the depth and spaciousness—the sheer abundance—of Wolfe's achievements. As he wrote, memory upon memory piled up, the thread of family connections grew longer and longer, the circle of experience wider and wider—as indeed it is bound to do if pursued far enough. And Wolfe was willing. Indeed, all his life he apparently was under a *compulsion* to do precisely that: *pursue and pursue all the interlocking and impinging relations and impressions that go into living a life*. He has been called an "elephantine Proust"; the quip is more just than most, except that Wolfe's forte was primarily descriptive and not analytic. In any case, it is as if from 1930 on, his reception gave Wolfe his calling and commitment. He would become the recorder of the American experience, in all its variety and amplitude. Wolfe frequently voices what could be construed and interpreted as nihilistic sentiments—certainly he sympathizes with the notion of an amoral, essentially "senseless" universe. Yet underlying his attitude toward experience is a faith that contradicts this view: at the root of his desire to devour experience is the notion that meaning resides there. His compulsion toward "more and more" is quickened by this faith, because it is allied with a feeling that one must not overlook an important aspect of "the meaning of things" that may lie uncovered within the next experience. Concealed in this view may be an incipient anti-intellectualism, in that it elevates the experiential mode of "knowing" above other modes of knowing. Too much, however, must not be made of this aspect of Wolfe, although it may seem to be one of those superficial links with Jack Kerouac which I spoke of earlier, and to which, therefore, I will return again later in this essay.

It is enough, for the moment, to remark the fact of Wolfe's commitment to this role as the epic bard of America and to show how he accommodated himself to the mantle. His second novel, *Of Time and the River* (1935), many years and millions of words in the making, carries forward the story of Eugene Gant. Like all his

3. Kennedy, *Window of Memory*, p. 192.

subsequent work, it is as autobiographical as his first book. Yet it is full of such passages as:

> For America has a thousand lights and weathers and we walk the streets, we walk the streets, we walk the streets forever, we walk the streets of life alone.
>
> It is the place of howling winds, the hurrying of the leaves in old October, the hard clean falling to the earth of acorns, the place of the storm-tossed moaning of the unity mountainside, where the young men cry out in their throats and feel the savage anger, the rude strong energies; the place also where the trains cross rivers.
>
> It is a fabulous county, the only fabulous county; it is the only place where miracles not only happen, but where they happen all the time.
>
> It is the place of exultancy and strong joy, the place of the darkened brooding air, the smell of snow; it is the place of all the fierce, the bitter colors in October, when all of the mild, sweet woods flame up; it is also the place of the cider press and the last brown oozings of the York Imperials. It is the place of the lovely girls with good jobs and the husky voices, who will buy a round of drinks; it is the place where the women with fine legs and silken underwear lie in the pullman berth below you; it is the place of the dark-green snore of the pullman cars, and the voices in the night-time in Virginia.
>
> It is the place where great boats are baying at the harbor's mouth, where great ships are putting out to sea; it is the place where great boats are blowing in the gulf of night, and where the river, the dark and secret river, full of strange time, is forever flowing by us to the sea.

Here we see, as one element, an apparent echo of Whitman's "barbaric yawp"—the celebration of young men crying out in their throats, the savage vigor, "the rude strong energies." There is the Whitmanesque intoxication with the raw experience of American life—the cataloging of its sights, sounds, smells, geography—and the narrator proclaiming his wonder, awe, and self-intoxicating awareness of the magnitude of it all (including himself as the chronicler).

And yet there are crucial differences, only suggested in the quoted passage, but developed elsewhere in the book and in his

later work. I am not of the school of thought which believes
Whitman to have been wholly devoid of an awareness of "evil,"
and whose reputation therefore suffered in America after the
Second World War, because he seemed to lack "a tragic sense of
life." Whitman, too, could say, "I was the man, I suffered. I was
there." In his life he bore witness to evil in his time as a nurse in the
Civil War, and his work includes "Out of the Cradle Endlessly
Rocking," "When Lilacs Last in the Dooryard Bloomed," and
other intimations of his knowledge of the dark places of human
experience. These endeavors by no means overshadow that other
Whitman of the "Song of Myself" and his more familiar image, but
they do not permit us too easy generalizations about him. It is,
however, finally a question of proportion—and in the propor-
tionate share of the tragic implications of life embodied in each
writer's work, we should have to say that Wolfe's work is more
consistently shaped by this awareness. The word "alone" in the
passage quoted is a portent, as is his fascination with "the dark and
secret river" (his image of life). In the midst of God's plenty, the
variety of American life, there is the lonely individual. Whereas in
Whitman this individual may presumably achieve communion and
rapport with the many and the "not-I," in a mystic release, in
Wolfe I think we perceive more forcefully the hunger of the individual to break through the isolation of self, but the continual
frustration of this effort. Instead of causing him to take stock, and
perhaps redirect his energies, this frustration only impels him
more and more ferociously toward cataloging, recording, and
hopelessly attempting to embrace all "otherness." No wonder
Wolfe's books drained him and ran to endless hundreds of thousands of words.

Isolation, finally, is for Wolfe the essence of man's tragic fate.
The quest for more and more, in the effort to break out of it, is
the old Romantic yearning for experience commensurate with the
infinite capacity to imagine, desire, and need. The quest is, of
course, doomed to failure and can end only with death. The quality of Wolfe that separates him from Whitman is precisely Wolfe's
awareness that this is so. This knowledge and self-knowledge
pervades his entire work. It gives to Wolfe's vision of America
a dual aspect: America is "the fabulous place," but it is also "the

place of violence and sudden death . . . it is the lawless land that feeds on murder." He produces, that is, full of contrarieties and paradoxes, a view in which good and evil are held in balanced suspension. He can say in the same sentence about America: "It is savage and cruel, but it is also the innocent place; it is the wild lawless place . . . but it is also the place of the child and laughter." The key to it all is his awareness that "we walk the streets, we walk the streets forever, we walk the streets of life alone" (both quotes from *Of Time and the River*). And in his last work, published posthumously, one of the most memorable sections begins with the observation that "the lives of men who have to live in our great cities are often tragically lonely." He then chronicles this loneliness in several vivid passages, but concludes, somewhat surprisingly, with an apostrophe to the promise of America:

> So, then, to every man his chance—to every man, regardless of his birth, his shining, golden opportunity—to every man the right to live, to work, to be himself, and to become whatever thing his manhood and his vision can combine to make him—this, seeker, is the promise of America. [*You Can't Go Home Again*]

This passage can be construed as a mere rhetorical gesture, an obeisance by Wolfe to his role, real or imagined, as the bard of the American experience. And yet, to those who know America, Wolfe seems to have caught at the essential element: that is, he expresses precisely the contradictory awareness of essential loneliness, the "isolate" in every man, combined with an "optative" mood. This paradox is at the heart of the American experience, and Wolfe deserves credit for his expression of it.

What about Kerouac's supposed relation to Wolfe? The comparison can be made because Kerouac often displays a "Wolfeian exuberance," a joy in experience, a delight in the sights, sounds, smells, geography of America, an apparently "Gargantuan gusto of life." On the surface, those would seem to be the qualities in these five selections from his best-known work, *On the Road* (1957):

> It was beautiful in Longmont. Under a tremendous old tree was a bed of green lawn-grass belonging to a gas station. I asked the attendant if I could sleep there, and he said sure; so I stretched out a wool shirt,

laid my face flat on it, with an elbow out, and with one eye looked at the snowy Rockies in the hot sun for just a moment. I fell asleep for two delicious hours, the only discomfort being an occasional Colorado ant. And here I am in Colorado! I kept thinking gleefully. Damn! damn! damn! I'm making it! And after a refreshing sleep filled with cobwebby dreams of my past life in the East I got up, washed in the station men's room, and strode off, fit and slick as a fiddle, and got me a rich thick milkshake at the roadhouse to put some freeze in my hot, tormented stomach.

At dusk we were coming into the humming streets of New Orleans. "Oh, smell the people!" yelled Dean with his face out the window, sniffing. "Ah! God! Life!" He swung around a trolley. "Yes." . . . the air was so sweet in New Orleans it seemed to come in soft bandannas; and you could smell the river and really smell the people, and mud, and molasses, and every kind of tropical exhalation with your nose suddenly removed from the dry ices of a Northern winter. We bounced in our seats. "And dig her!" yelled Dean, pointing at another woman. "Oh, I love, love, love women! I think women are wonderful! I love women!" He spat out the window; he groaned; he clutched his head. Great beads of sweat fell from his forehead from pure excitement and exhaustion.

[In Nebraska Sal Paradise, the narrator, hears a happy farmer laugh and says:] Wham, listen to that man laugh, that's the West, here I am in the West. He came booming into the diner, calling Maw's name, and she made the sweetest cherry pie in Nebraska, and I had some with a mountainous scoop of ice-cream on top. It was the spirit of the West sitting right next to me. . . . Whooee, I told my soul. . . .

[And then, as if to underline the aspect of celebration, Kerouac offers an invocation to the great brown god, the Mississippi, and a magical listing of American place names:] On rails we leaned and looked at the great brown father of waters rolling down from mid-America like the torrent of broken souls—bearing Montana logs and Dakota muds and Iowa vales and things that had drowned in Three Forks, where the secret began in ice.

[We have also the magical listing of names linked with the legendary heroes of America:] I thought all the wilderness of America was in the West till the Ghost of the Susquehanna showed me different. No, there is a wilderness in the East; it's the same wilderness Ben Franklin plodded in the oxcart days when he was postmaster, the same as it was when George Washington was a wild-buck Indian fighter, when Daniel Boone told stories by Pennsylvania lamps and promised to find the Gap, when Bradford built his road and men whooped her up in log cabins. There were no great Arizona spaces for the little man, just the bushy wilderness of eastern Pennsylvania, Maryland, and Virginia, the backwoods, the black-tar roads that curve along the mournful rivers like Susquehanna, Monongahela, old Potomac and Monocacy.

Surely, in these examples we detect affinities with Whitman and Wolfe: the pleasure in naming, in the senses, in people, in what Whitman called in *Democratic Vistas* the outstanding features of our political life—"variety and freedom." At what then do I cavil, and why do I suggest there is no serious identification here with Wolfe? When we recall that Allen Ginsberg dedicated *Howl*—that splendid poem which began much of the interest in the Beats—to Kerouac (among others), whom he extolled for "creating a spontaneous bop prosody," we approach the essential point of difference. Ginsberg, that is, calls our attention to Kerouac's *language*. Once that is done, we may perceive essential differences in Wolfe's and Kerouac's conception of language and with it, inevitably, in their conception of the experience to be named and embodied by language.

First of all, Kerouac is not really interested in true naming, for that is an act of definition—an act of discrimination. When all experience is reduced to the same level, and elicits the same sort of response, there is no discrimination. Kerouac's is a more primitive impulse; and indeed, as Ginsberg called it, a "spontaneous" one. Kerouac's tendency is merely to *point* to or indicate an experience, and either drop it entirely or merely exclaim at it with no effort at intellection at all. That is the heart of the matter. "Wham," "Ah," "Whooee," he exclaims, and then no more—or, rather, then he goes off for a milkshake or an ice-cream, precisely a childish response to experience. The food for the mind in these passages is insubstantial, and full only of quick and illusory energy. And how to respond to his use of geography and history? What he trots out in these passages may be acquired in the fifth grade of even the most impoverished educational background. And it is not as if Kerouac, who after all attended Columbia University, did not know better. No, it represents, I think, a deliberate rejection of sophistication. The appeal of the Beats lies, to some extent, in exactly this: that they reject those artifices of intelligence that seemed in their time to rob experience of the richness inherent in it. They apparently believed in reducing stimulus and response to the simplest level, thereby reinvigorating the capacity to respond wholly to experience. They hoped to restore vigor to the life of feeling by reacting spontaneously. Thought, complication of language, discrimination, are seen to get in the way. Now in some respects this is not so unusual or even reprehensible a theory—and in practice did usher in a rich popular literature, free of boring academic fussiness. It can be a powerful stimulus toward refreshing literature. In parts, it seems not far from some of the formulations of Wordsworth in his preface to the *Lyrical Ballads*. But Wordsworth hoped to enrich his language, not, as in the results shown in the passages taken from *On the Road*, to impoverish it. "Wham," "Whee," and "Ah" do not enrich anything. Although they may point to the existence of some kind of feeling, there is no attempt to render it (I revert to the Jamesian word, from "The Art of Fiction"), objectify it, present it to the reader. Literature is made with words, not feelings. The mistiness of "Damn, damn, damn, I'm making it!" may express exuberance, but little else. Making *what*, I find myself asking, and when the answer isn't the equally vague "It," it usually comes to me as "Sound." Sound is not literature, although it may surely be "spontaneous"; it cannot be, in my view, quite the same in literature as the spontaneity and creativity of bop or jazz sound.

And therein is the essential difference from Thomas Wolfe; whatever his faults, poverty of language is not one of them, nor is mere spontaneity of response his goal. In his most gushing and seemingly uncritical moments, we nevertheless sense a tradition at work in Wolfe. His chanting rhetoric may derive from an oral tradition, from the Bible, and very often from his reading of the Elizabethans. The point is that even at his worst we perceive conscious artifice at work. Though I suggested earlier that there is an incipient anti-intellectualism possible in his attitude toward experience, it is tempered in a way to make it markedly different from Kerouac's. Wolfe goes on to say that Webber hoped to "wring" the meaning from his experience, and that an important element in it was Webber's ability to "reflect" on it. Furthermore, reading in books was included in the world of experience, and *their* meanings were to be wrung from them. Wolfe talks of the importance of "the depth and intensity" with which he experiences things (*The Story of a Novel*, p. 47), but this should not be interpreted as merely extolling feelings, for thought and reflection were indispensable ways of extending depth and feeling.

Wolfe's hope, he wrote in *The Story of a Novel* (1936), was "to make a living thing out of the substances of his one life," and his effort was to find the language which would enable him to do that (p. 49). Wolfe's intentions, in short, were seriously those of a literary artist. As he said, the lists and the hundreds and thousands of words he poured into his ledgers and manuscripts were purposeful explorations. Those lists of towns and cities, descriptions, as he wrote, of "springs, wheels, flanges, axle rods, color, weight, and quality of the day coach of an American railway train . . . the color and design of the wallpaper, the way a towel hung down, the way a chair creaked" (pp. 42–43), were, he knew, part of an "intemperate excess, an almost insane hunger to devour the entire body of human experience" (p. 46). But they were *purposeful* explorations in which the aim was to make these explorations accurate and evocative, so that Wolfe, as well as the reader, could say, yes, that was the thing, the whole truth of the experience.

In addition to the traditions that may be perceived as affecting Wolfe's work, there was his three-year apprenticeship in the difficult craft of playwriting at Baker's "47 Workshop" at Harvard. This, coupled with his practice of discarding long manuscripts that he thought were lacking in craft, undermine the view that he was a wholly undisciplined "natural." He was no untutored genius or half-wit, warbling native woodnotes wild. He says, at least, that he did not write as some people thought he did. In a famous letter to F. Scott Fitzgerald, he drew an amusing, imaginary picture of "a man as a great 'exuberant' six-foot-six clod-hopper straight out of nature who bites off half a plug of apple tobacco, tilts the corn liquor jug and lets half of it gurgle down his throat, wipes off his mouth with the back of one heavy paw, jumps three feet in the air and clacks his heels together four times before he hits the floor again and yells out 'Whoopee, boys, I'm a rootin', tootin', shootin' son of a gun from Buncombe County—out of my way now, here I come!'—and then wads up three-hundred thousand words or so, hurls it at a blank page, puts covers on it and says 'Here's my book!' " Nobody, as he told Scott Fitzgerald, ever did it that way, and although, as he also said in that letter, he was a "putter-inner" rather than a "taker-outer," he was also attempting to be more restrained, to be more "selective," to be a better artist, but to do it in his own way.[4]

But all this can be discounted as intention and biography—the test, of course, is the work. And here, we must admit, the achievement often belied the intention. There is no question that Wolfe could be drearily repetitious, that too often he merely lists rather than renders experience, that his rhetoric and chants merely vaporize what he is trying to describe, that his Eugene Gant and George Webber behave often like Dean Moriarity—raging, ranting, spitting, head-clutching, and the rest. But at his best, and he frequently is at his best, he could, as H. J. Muller puts it *render* his emotion, with a wealth of precise detail, "correctly and dramatically":

> The lights burn, the electric signs wink and flash, the place is still horribly intact in all its bleak prognathous newness, but all the people are dead, gone, vanished. The place is a tomb of frozen silence, as terrifying in its empty bleakness as those advertising backshops we saw formerly in theaters, where the splendid buildings, stores, and shops of a great street are painted in the richest and most flattering colors, and where there is no sign of life whatever.

Passages such as these, and there are many, "contribute," as Muller says, "to the blazing pageantry of Wolfe's novels, by which he evokes more vividly and fully than any other American writer, the look, sound and feel of American life. . . . These passages,

4. *The Letters of Thomas Wolfe*, ed. Elizabeth Nowell (New York: Scribners, 1956), pp. 641–45.

moreover, are not merely striking backdrops: they are the living stage, inseparable from the drama. They are the concrete substance of the American myth, whose central meaning Wolfe was seeking."[5]

It is in the magnitude of Wolfe's seeking that I think his permanent value resides. His is a unique position in American letters: his method and peculiar achievement are not of the kind that are exemplary for other writers; indeed they may be harmful in their seeming celebrations of mere size and energy and extensive concentration on "experience." But I think as a last word we can go to William Faulkner, undoubtedly the greatest American writer of his century. When asked to "rate" his contemporaries, Faulkner gave "first place" to Thomas Wolfe, because although he failed—as all writers must according to Faulkner—to achieve the vision and ideal he had, he nevertheless set himself the greatest and most difficult task of all his contemporaries.

5. H. J. Muller, *Thomas Wolfe* (New York: New Directions, 1947), pp. 41–42.

Nine

Styron's *Sophie's Choice:*
Jews and Other Marginals

First of all, I want to comment on the announced title of this essay when it was first conceived as a paper.[1] It was originally supposed to be called "The Cultural Politics of Southern and Jewish Writers"—which is a fine title and subject, but it is of course much too broad and requires book-length treatment. If I were to write such a book, I would be concerned with the energies and strategies used by key writers representative of these groups—which I would consider paradigmatic for regional, ethnic, and other "marginal" phenomena in American culture—as they launched an assault upon, infiltrated, charmed, or recast the mold and idea of the national literature.

Taken as groups, it is obvious enough that Southern and Jewish writers have moved from a kind of marginality earlier in the century—and it is *that* category of marginality, rather than their definition regionally or ethnically that matters for the purpose of this analysis—to positions of recognized achievement and importance in the literary world of the forties, fifties, sixties, and the present.

If I were to do an ambitious study of just how this was achieved, I would be interested to learn how these writers (often in masked

1. The paper was delivered at the American Studies Association Meeting, 31 October 1981, for the "Regionalism and Ethnicity in American Literature" panel.

form) became part of the dominant culture to which they aspired; what the stakes were for group and personal validation, or what they were perceived to be; also, what the advantages were of this validation, and what its effect was upon ontological and metaphysical being; and certainly how the process modified ideas and values.

Such a study would proceed along two lines, parallel at times, intersecting at others. First, there would be the close reading of chief literary texts in which highly charged resonances concerning marginality could be discerned. Second, I would study some of the chief cultural instruments through which the "outsiders" identified themselves and their targets, and how the various conflicts were thereby mediated.

To take the second first, I would look at the Fugitives group, historically and in their publications, and read through the *Sewanee Review* in the twenties and thirties and the *Southern Review* in the thirties. The emergence of Southern agrarians and other writers should be seen in relation to Southern issues and arguments, then against the background of the New Deal and international problems as well as in their specifically literary concerns. Balancing this exploration would be a look at the *Menorah Journal* of the twenties and the *Partisan Review* of the thirties and forties, in which the literary, social, and political values of a secular, urban, largely Jewish intelligentsia were worked out and legitimated.

One would also study the book pages of the *New York Times* and *Herald-Tribune*, the *New Republic* and *Nation;* the publishing industry; the work of "culture critics" like Randolph Bourne, Lewis Mumford, and Waldo Frank; the careers of relevant actors in the drama who moved into positions of academic, publishing, and other forms of cultural influence.

It would be a fascinating and back-breaking study—which I am glad to say I am not going to do at this time. Nor am I going to do more than name some of the Jewish and Southern writers one would have to consider in such a study. Among Jewish writers, I would start with Abraham Cahan, roughly contemporaneous with George Washington Cable and with him one of the "progenitors," and end, of course, with a long look at Bellow, Malamud, and Philip Roth.

Among Southern writers I might begin with Cable and *The*

Grandissimes and end with Styron's *Sophie's Choice*. Along the way I would think hard about Faulkner, Thomas Wolfe, Robert Penn Warren, and others—seen from the perspective of their concern with moving from the provincial to the metropolitan (literally and/or figuratively), from the regional to the universal, and with their treatment of the life-and-death struggle between tradition and modernity.

A very large order, indeed. Let me, therefore, get down at last to the simpler subject of my talk and this essay: "Styron's *Sophie's Choice*, read as a Southern writer's view of himself in relation to the center of American literature, and how he might occupy it" (not to say, crudely, "take it over"). Or, a reasonable subtitle might be: "Styron, Jews, and Other Marginals, and the Mainstream."

Succinctly put, my thesis in relation to all this is that Styron commits an audacious act of symbolic and imaginative appropriation, mediating between the traditional center of American literature and culture and that of the challenging marginals or provincials, creating the image of where *he* stands as the enlarged, augmented, new real center. Like Ishmael in *Moby Dick* (on page 1, Styron's narrator says, "Call me Stingo"), Styron's fictionalized and mythicized self is the only one left alive at the end of the novel to tell its story. For Melville's isolatoes federated along a single keel who went down with the ship, substitute that other cross-section of interesting types whom Styron kills in the novel: Nathan Landau, the breezy, brilliant Jew (a cross between Lenny Bruce, Norman Mailer, and scores of other talented, word-spinning Jews who would come over from Brooklyn to transform American culture); Sophie, the Polish Auschwitz survivor, a doomed mother who has seen hell but also enjoys—or at least participates in—fanciful sex; and in the background two slaves, the fictional Artiste whose sale down the river provides Stingo with a small financial legacy that enables him to explore life among the Jews in Brooklyn and thus develop as a writer, and of course Nat Turner, who keeps popping up in this novel in the damndest places. Styron is obviously not finished with Turner until he proves that he had been thinking seriously about Turner for more than twenty years before the black writers' response to his *Confessions of Nat Turner* (1967) challenged him on the issue. Jews, women, blacks.

To move to another paradigm, Styron/Stingo is the young man

from the provinces arriving at and trying to make it in (or conquer) the center of the culture—for Styron/Stingo, the literary culture. The book opens on that theme, and in my reading it is the key to comprehending the various themes, strategies, styles, and modes of the book. It is a very literary book, or at least very self-consciously a writer's book, including lists of other writers; discussions of the literary marketplace; footnotes in the text to source material on Auschwitz and on Southern populism; and the future course of American literature (a key debate involves Nathan informing Stingo, in 1947, that the Southern domination of American writing will be supplanted by that of Jewish writers—and when pressed for an example, Nathan comes up precociously with a young writer named Saul Bellow). Styron also parodies or one-ups his competition among Southern writers (like Faulkner and Wolfe) and among Jewish writers (like Philip Roth—as in the long comic gem of the novel, the description of Stingo's encounter with the supreme Brooklyn tease Leslie Lapidus). There is something in this also reminiscent of John Updike's achievement and put-downs of the stereotypical Jewish ethnic and intellectual novelist in *Bech: A Book*.

The young provincial's first job, fresh from a traditional Duke literary education, is at McGraw-Hill on 42nd Street—in those halcyon post–World War II days sure to be seen as the very heart of things by the unhip, whose version of the center of New York life derived from World War II newsreels. Stingo quickly comes to realize that McGraw-Hill's flashy building is in actuality "a spiritually enervating green tower," and he must strike out for freedom and greener pastures. Before getting fired for floating plastic bubbles that look suspiciously like blown-up condoms, he seeks imaginative release by brandishing a copy of the *New York Post*—called by some over the years the English version of the *Jewish Daily Forward*—around the staid, basically WASP offices. For good measure he flashes the *Daily Worker*, which enables him, he says, to play the dual role of "imaginary Communist and fictive Jew." It ain't what you do, or what you are, but an image, created by what you read, or at least know about. References to the *New Republic* and *Partisan Review*, those other organs of the New York intelligentsia, are also tossed about. The disguise put on by Stingo also emphasizes that only "a fictive Jew" could pass over the threshold and inhabit the office—even the relatively lowly one held by Stingo. Discharged, he must also leave his room in Greenwich Village, that other assumed center of literary culture. From his window there he had fantasized literary garden parties with Wallace Stevens, Robert Lowell, Faulkner, Huxley, Cheever, and others of the high literary culture to which he aspires. These parties were to be held in the yard across the way belonging to an enticingly back-sided woman he names (to himself) Mavis Hunnicutt. The garden of literary and sensuous, sexual delights are always thus conjoined in the book. Doubly rejected, he moves East of Eden, to Yetta Zimmerman's pink bower (and womb) of a rooming house in Flatbush, deep in the heart of Brooklyn. There he is to earn his bread (and literary fame) by the sweat of his brow, working on the novel that is to become *Lie Down in Darkness*.

This eastern province of Manhattan is of course, in 1947, the year of the novel's setting, the launching pad for a vital new cultural force ready to burst on the scene: Jewish energy, Jewish humor, Jewish literary achievement.[2] Brooklyn, Kings County (even a step up on the royalty charts from Duke U), "the Kingdom of the Jews," as Styron calls it on page one. He goes over, a raider from or of the lost ark, to find the true word with which he can go back for his real raid on the established center of American culture. He will inhabit this new kingdom for a period of time, grow in knowledge and experience from his adventures and the opportunities there, and then return to his old community, fit for leadership.

Victor Turner's useful differentiation between liminality and marginality can be applied to the pattern I am describing. The liminal condition—the strategy of placing people outside the boundaries of the town or the culture to experience both anxiety and freedom, new states of being; engaging in a version of misrule that will both purge them of antisocial needs as well as enlarge their base of experience in the achievement of a new spiritual "communion"—is of course the prelude to coming back in and being ac-

2. See the sociologically important chapter 4, in Albert Goldman's *Ladies and Gentlemen—Lenny Bruce!!* (New York: Random House, 1974), entitled "How Sick Humor Came up the River from Brooklyn to Manhattan, along the Gowanus Parkway (42nd Street Exit)," for one aspect of this cultural change.

cepted by the community (a version, but with significant differences, of what we used to think of as rites of passage). But that
does not mean that in the so-called primitive societies studied by
Turner (and others) there weren't/aren't real marginals. There
were crazies—bad women and God knows what else, which had to
be permanently excluded—whose absolute otherness could not be
mediated or made socially functional within the community.[3]
They do not come back in and win acceptance and significant
places for the communities they have established in their marginal
states. For Styron/Stingo, the Southern writer is liminal, not truly
marginal. He is only one more "lean and lonesome young Southerner wandering amid the Kingdom of the Jews." From this wandering, as I read it, he will take or absorb what is of value and return to the main line to tell the tale. What he achieves in Brooklyn
is (1) a breakthrough to his true literary subject, (2) important face-
to-face "communitas"-establishing encounters with Nathan and
Sophie, and (3) the promise of sexual fulfillment; a holy trinity—
sex, career, the Jewish fate. Of course at the end the desired sex object—Sophie—chooses the Jew over him, but he has the last word
(after his tears, Stingo prints his own poem), because in choosing
Nathan she chooses death.

What Styron aspires to is a firm link with the main line of the
American novel, the tradition, as Paul Fussell has pointed out, that
includes *The Portrait of a Lady* and *The Great Gatsby*, in which the
theme of an American innocent's confrontation with great evil and
his/her complicity in it is explored. Jews, blacks, and women remain the real marginals, assimilated to the great line only by
Styron's kind of appropriation of their domain, legitimating their
experience at the augmented and higher level that his work provides. Styron tries to have his cake and eat it too, in other ways as
well. First, he retains his Southernness, claims his place in the line
of his immediate great ancestors—chiefly Faulkner and Wolfe—
and the advantages that thereby accrue to his sensibility, though
subtly supplanting them because of his contemporary superhip-

3. And Turner cites women, especially. See Victor Turner, *Drama, Fields, and
Metaphors: Symbolic Action in Human Society* (Ithaca, N.Y.: Cornell University Press,
1974), p. 255.

ness about such things as New York, fancy sex, and the literary scene. Then he touches base with and absorbs the energies of the most vital strains in the contemporary period. By the end of chapter five, he has mastered *The Portable Faulkner* and the cuisine at Himmelfarb's Delux Delicatessen—an unbeatable combination! The end product is a claim to major status as an American writer. (I am deliberately putting aside all considerations about Auschwitz in the book, and concomitant dark broodings on guilt and evil— which may suggest a bid for major international and even "universal" status, although I suspect it is heavy freight mainly on the American scene.) It is the American cultural significance of Styron's literary strategy on which I am focusing.

I want to suggest yet another way to go at this question of regionalism and its literary significance. Some years ago, following Larzer Ziff's lead in *The American 1890s* on this question, I simply assumed that many of the writers relegated to the regional or local color rubric were victims of an injustice—being denied their true significance. Their real concerns were frequently much more serious than to reveal the wonderful diversity in American life, or the basic homogeneity that lay beneath the appearance of divergence. I tried to show, therefore, that Cable, Cahan, Kate Chopin, Charles Chesnutt, were actually dealing with the great questions of their day—race, class, acculturation of vast immigrant populations, radical shifts in sexual values and mores—and that to consider them as regionalists, as the term was generally understood, was obfuscation. Reflecting along these lines on Styron's strategy of using a regional identity and imaginative landscape from which to make raids upon the imaginative terrain of other regions, and on his being unusually sensitive to the *moment* and *milieu*—by which I mean his sense of the literary audience and the literary situation in a period of cultural uncertainty and change—I was led to thinking about that other great Southern writer, perhaps our first truly *American* writer, Mark Twain, and *his* sense of these things.

Twain was a master at inventing and juggling regional personae. He adopted whatever mask was necessary to mediate among the various regional landscapes, appropriating them to his imagination, and in the process creating an imaginative center that represented a new cultural synthesis. One has simply to cite some of his

poses to make the point. In *Roughing It* he pretends to be an effete
Easterner at the beginning of his journey to Nevada and California, bemoaning the fact that there will be no need for his white
tie and top hat at Pawnee receptions; or the tenderfoot tricked by
the knowing Westerner into buying "a genuine Mexican plug."
And so forth, simply not mentioning his growing up in Missouri or
the years on the Mississippi, because of the fictive requirements of
the tale he invents. And Twain was accepted by Eastern audiences, eager for news from the West, as it were, a taste already
cultivated by Bret Harte and others. Or later for his rediscovery of
the Mississippi Valley, and his making it—definitively and for all
time in *Huckleberry Finn*—the very center of an American identity.
One could go on at length on this theme of Twain's manipulations
and adaptations of regional expectations, conscious always of the
audience, and drawing upon his contacts with so many diverse elements, classes, and regions of American life, as well as his shifts of
literary personae: in the West an Easterner; for the East a rough
diamond from the coast. And his actual geographical mobility
might be noted—his residence in Hartford, midway between
Boston and New York (and *that* shift of a center and emphasis in
America's cultural life is itself suggestive) and his residence for so
many years abroad, loving England and Germany, but pretending
for the market to be tweaking the lion's nose (in *Connecticut Yankee*)
or mocking the impossible German language. He did not always
negotiate with perfect success the tensions and fiction attendant
upon creating himself as the center of an American cultural identity—as Henry Nash Smith showed so cogently in his analysis of
Twain's (and Howells's) responses to the Whittier birthday
speech.[4] On that occasion, as you will recall, his barely contained,
or even barely understood, ambivalence toward the official culture—embodied in the venerable sages of the old New England
tradition—when confronted by an image of the roughneck West
almost undid him. Or, at least at the end of that interesting story,
the person called Mark Twain cannot answer when the easily
fooled California miner asks him if he, too, isn't an imposter?

4. Henry Nash Smith, *Mark Twain: The Development of a Writer* (Cambridge:
Harvard University Press, 1972), pp. 56–72.

I suppose it is a question that has occurred to more than one American writer, for reasons that go deep into the shifting and fluid bases of our culture. And I wonder if it does not occur with particular force to one who dons, or is made to don, a regional or ethnic identity. Nobody is a regionalist or an ethnic in their primary conception of themselves all the time—that goes without saying. A person/writer would be a monster if it *were* the case. Much of what I have said about Styron might be construed as being somewhat derogatory—that there might be something too opportunistic or self-serving about his literary strategy, or that there is less to the book than at first thought. I do not mean my analysis to be taken in this way. For one thing, the dust of evaluation has by no means settled on this book, and judging from the strength and division of opinion in the great number of serious reviews it drew, it is both an important book and not an easy one to judge conclusively. For example, Doris Grumbach, Paul Fussell, John Gardner, and Larzer Ziff think *Sophie's Choice* is a masterpiece, or at least a major work; other serious critics—Walter Goodman, Robert Towers, Julian Symonds in *TLS*—think it a colossal failure, bombastic, melodramatic; others don't know what to think (*Commentary*); a few—the best, in my view—like Leslie Fiedler and Robert Alter say very intelligent things about its relation to Jews, and neither overpraise nor overcondemn. In short, there may be a need at this point in the book's career for some preliminary notes like mine toward a serious study of it seen from any number of vantage points. My point is to use the book to call attention, chiefly, to a perhaps necessary way a writer can become an American writer. It *always* requires an audacious and appropriating act of the imagination. One of the ways is to raid a popular or strong genre or position, shake it for all it's worth, extract what you can, then rise above or out of it, or use and transcend the limitations of region, or ethnic, gender, or class particularity (as is a fashionable way to put it). I happen to think it is only through such particularities that one can even approach such a thing as universality (Joyce's Dublin in *Ulysses* comes immediately to mind).

Closer to home, think what Philip Roth did with *Portnoy's Complaint*: among other things, he polished off the sentimental Yiddishe momma theme or genre as a possible subject, once and for all. In Roth's fine book *The Ghost Writer* (1979)—in which he imagines Anne Frank alive and the mistress of his self-absorbed master, the writer Lonoff—he has applied the final Jamesian turn of the screw upon ethnic themes and the ethnic writer generally. After that, Roth's work suggests, I submit, that, Jewish American writer though he is, there are no categories, only the imagination, and writing.

In a sense, and in summary, that is what I think Styron has attempted, with the materials he found to hand, in his last book. Sacvan Bercovitch has shown us in his usual brilliant and persuasive way "How the Puritans Won the American Revolution," and how, among other things, they rather than some other group set their stamp indelibly on American culture (so, for example, Thanksgiving is *the* American holiday, and not, say, Virginia Dare Day). The means they used and that are always used were audacious and strong acts of the imagination (texts) along with control or at least access to key organs of culture necessary for spreading the word.[5]

And so, I have come back to the main point in the outline I presented at the beginning of this essay. The way to study and understand the movement of Southern and Jewish writers from positions of marginality toward centrality is to study their strong texts and the ways they gained social access to the institutions of cultural dominance. One would hope that the history of those others whom Styron seems to regard as still marginal—blacks and women—will prove that they are actually in a liminal position, on the threshold of real entry to and possession of their share of the center of our collective American lives.

5. Sacvan Bercovitch, "How the Puritans Won the American Revolution," *Massachusetts Review* 17 (Winter 1976): 597–630.

Index